Water ME NEXT WEEK
A *Succulent's* PLEA

BEGINNERS GUIDE TO WATERING SUCCULENTS

Theresa Jimeno Ebro

For permission contact:
chopstickandsucculents@gmail.com

Designer:
Ma Theresa Ebro

Photographers:
Benjamin Ramos
Enrico Esteban
Ma Theresa Ebro

Editor:
Qat Wanders
Wandering Words Media

Proofreader:
Allison Rose Goddard

Logo Design:
Jane Ramos Cox

ISBN 978-1-7345736-0-2

Visit our Web site:
www.chopstickandsucculents.com

Notes
The information in this book is
based on the author's experiences and
lessons learned as she worked with succulents in her
garden. Research conducted from reliable online
sources and local libraries is also included.
This book is a product of the author's fondness for
succulents and devotion to guiding beginners to successfully
grow drought-smart plants.
Most of the succulents specified are the soft succulents
used for creating arrangements.

Water ME NEXT WEEK

A *Succulent's* PLEA

BEGINNERS GUIDE TO WATERING SUCCULENTS

START YOUR HOBBY RIGHT BY UNDERSTANDING THE
UNIQUENESS OF SUCCULENTS AND THE SPECIAL WAY
THEY HANDLE WATER

To those who are new to succulents.
To those who tried growing succulents and failed.
To those who are puzzled by the unique way they handle *water*.

A Poem from *Echeveria*

There is something you need to know about me,
I am different from other plants,
I have the capacity to store water,
That's what made me so unique among others.

I can also conserve water efficiently,
So, replenishing my supply is not always necessary.
I can take care of myself,
Even if you sometimes neglect me,
The next time you check, I will still look lovely.

I have a love-hate relationship with water,
I love to sip and keep it,
But I hate that I have no self-control,
I cannot resist sipping even when I am so full.

So please, when you give me water, kindly check me first,
If I look bloated, that means I don't thirst,
Also, soaking my feet is not a good idea
Because I always want it dry and I hate foot spas.

Echeveria

To my parents, Raymundo and Rebecca, who brought me up on the farm.
To my husband, Eryl, who understands and supports my addiction to succulents.
To all my family, friends, and co-workers, whose kind and encouraging words inspired me.

Table Of Contents

Discovering A New Passion

INTRODUCTION
Discovering A New Passion

Succulents are fascinating plants. They have the reputation of being resilient and easy to grow and maintain. But that isn't always what everyone experiences when they first get one.

While it is true that succulents are tough, they can also become delicate and hard to please. This can happen when they are watered the same way as non-drought-tolerant plants.

The most common reason why growing succulents fails is overwatering.

Of all the mistakes one can commit when growing succulents, overwatering should be the number one to avoid because its effects happen quickly and are the most deadly.

Some succulents can elongate when placed indoors without adequate lighting. But this won't kill them fast. You can even take advantage of the result and grow your collection by propagating new succulents from their leaves and fast-growing stems. But combining lack of sunlight with too much water will result in succulents' early demise.

They can get sunburned when exposed to harsh sunlight abruptly. Yes, this may sound a bit confusing, since succulents are native to areas where they are exposed to the extreme heat of the sun all day. The reason they get sunburned is when they are not allowed to acclimatize.

Although sun damage is irreversible, succulents can outgrow it over time. But the combination of overwatering and sunburn will result in a mushy succulent with squishy black leaves—an ugly sight with almost no hope for survival.

When succulents are overwatered, their cells are damaged from the inside. When not detected early, the plant may die fast.

There is a lot of opposing advice when it comes to watering succulents. If you go online for your succulent-care needs, you probably have noticed that the more you search, the more confusing it gets.

Some say they water their succulents twice a week, while others water twice a month. Some soak their plants in water, but some give just a few drops. Some say that misting is not good, while others swear it's how they kept their succulents alive.

What's even more confusing is when you see dying plants revived to good health with water therapy by soaking its bare roots in water for a few days.

Isn't that quite puzzling?

While some people are struggling to avoid overwatering, others soak the bare roots in water. When you are shown how plump and healthy a plant looks twenty-four hours after so-called water therapy, it's easy to be tempted to do the same. But when you try the same technique and fail, it will not only frustrate you but also confuse you. If you are not persistent enough, you'll end up giving up this amazing hobby.

But once you understand how succulents handle water, all these confusing situations will become clear.

Remember, not all the tips you read online about watering succulents are right.

At least, not all of that advice is right for your succulent plants. One method might have worked for others' plants, but that method might be harmful to yours.

Do you know why?

Because you might not have the same succulent plants, and if you do, the plants may not be the same size. You also likely do not have the same soil mixture, and even if you do, containers can vary.

Your succulents might be indoors. Theirs might be outdoors, soaking up more sun than yours is inside. And then there's the environment; your humidity and temperature levels are probably different, too.

A succulent's species and its size, soil mixture, container, sunlight exposure, temperature and humidity levels matter. All these factors can affect the amount of water your succulents need—and how often they need it.

But what are succulents, anyway? Why does growing them seem so easy for others, but complicated to some?

Succulents are plants that store water in their leaves, roots, or stems. Let's make it even simpler: *they store water*. That description alone can tell us what makes them different from other plants.

The water they absorb is the very reason why they can survive in areas where water is scarce. Their stored water can sustain them for several weeks, or even months.

Their changing of colors, waxy coatings, cobwebby hairs, and flour-like coatings are there for a reason— to protect them from the harsh heat of the sun and keep their surface area moist, or to keep insects away. The more you understand the uniqueness of these plants, the more you'll realize how special they are.

It is also worth knowing that although all succulents store water, they do not all handle it the same way. Some can save more, while others can only hold a small amount at a time. Some can go for more extended periods without being watered, while others will show signs of need.

To be successful in growing them, you need to understand how water plays an essential role in their existence.

But succulents don't just store water. Succulents are good at conserving and protecting their supply. Most of their unique features are their adaptive ways of saving and protecting their stored water.

Although all succulents store water, they do not all handle it the same way. Some can save more, while others can only hold a small amount at a time. Some can go for more extended periods without being watered, while others will show signs of need.

To be successful in growing them, you need to understand how water plays an essential role in their existence.

Photographer: Benjamin Ramos

The Gift

First Project

Who am I, and why should you learn from me?

Seven years ago, I was a beginner like you—confused and worried that I would not be capable of caring for the succulent arrangement I received as a gift. Sure enough, half of them died the first time I watered them.

My name is Theresa Ebro. I grew up in the Philippines, and I am a farmer's daughter. As a child, I watched in awe of how my parents grew different varieties of vegetables from seeds.

I've been a nurse for twenty-five years, and even though I grew up on a farm, I never worked on it. But my father's blood—the blood of a farmer—runs in me. A tiny seed he planted in my heart during childhood silently grew within me, waiting for that perfect time to bloom. From that seed emerged a love of growing plants. Not vegetables, but succulents.

I now live in California, 2.7 miles away from Disneyland. Our climate is mild to hot year-round and mostly dry. We enjoy a subtropical Mediterranean climate with seasonal changes in rainfall, which means dry summers and rainy winters.

Overall, it's the best weather to grow succulents. I am truly blessed to have found this hobby.

I will not forget the day I created my first succulent arrangement.

It was a warm summer evening in 2016. I came home tired after working a twelve-hour shift. The back of my neck was stiff, my arms were heavy, and my legs were sore. My whole body was as tired as my worn-out duty shoes.

We had our dinner in the garden that night. When it was over, I decided to linger and elevate my feet on a patio chair. While I was relaxing, an empty terra-cotta pot caught my eye. Whatever plant that was growing in there did not survive the drought we were facing that year.

A month before, my husband, Eryl, and I visited one of the mission churches in Oceanside, California. It was there in Mission San Luis Rey that I laid eyes on the most colorful succulents I've ever seen, arranged in containers of different sizes, in wreaths, and in repurposed items.

I fell in love with them at once, not because it was the first time I saw those kinds of plants, but because I realized I had some of those plants growing in my garden for years. I didn't know how beautiful they could become when used in miniature landscapes. Mine were neglected in our backyard, growing big and mostly green. How the staff managed to keep their succulents small and colorful intrigued me.

The old fountain arrangement was my absolute favorite. It held a miniature landscape with a small replica of the church. Rocks added interest to the design, with small pebbles used to depict a pathway through a garden of succulent plants. It displayed a living art that told a story. While staring at it, I felt a sense of excitement to build my own succulent scene one day. I looked at it closely, as if trying to dissect every layer of it, imprinting the design, the materials, and the plant varieties used in my mind.

When we got home from vacation, I bought what I needed for the project. Small embellishments, different-colored pebbles and sands, cactus soil, and a few more low-growing succulents. I was hoping to create an arrangement that week. Of course, it never happened.

For almost a month, the items I bought were in a corner, waiting patiently for me to find the time.

That evening was a perfect time. While staring at an empty terracotta pot, the vision of those beautiful arrangements returned to me. I felt so excited. I got up and went to work on it. I played around like a little kid, touching the dirt with my hand, adding one plant at a time.

I was alone that night in the garden, and it was quiet. I concentrated so hard on what I was doing that I completely forgot about my long, stressful day.

Engrossed in that moment, enjoying every piece I added to the pot, I saw the empty container transform into the arrangement I visualized. And something changed within me.

I felt so light and relaxed.

My tensed muscles softened.

I felt renewed energy.

There was an unexplained feeling of happiness and excitement.

I asked myself, "Didn't I just have a long day?"

Working with succulents didn't feel like working at all—it felt like playing! I had stumbled upon an activity that made me feel like a kid again. I had found a hobby that allowed me to be creative while also providing myself with peace and comfort I had been searching for. It allowed me to disconnect from technology and slow down.

The feeling was so addicting. From that day on, I was packing the car with succulents. I arranged them in different-sized containers, fountains, bird feeders, baskets, wreaths, and frames—the possibilities were endless. For the first time, I found a hobby that I was passionate about and that made me happy.

Since then, visiting nurseries in search of new varieties has become my ongoing quest. But I don't just collect, I arrange them. Creating arrangements has become my pastime. It is the most relaxing activity that I always look forward to doing.

When creating arrangements, using cuttings is easier than those with roots. I cut a portion from the mother plant, remove the bottom leaves, and use the cuttings. This led me to discover new things. I knew you could encourage new sprouts to grow from trimmed plants, but I never expected a single leaf to grow a new plant!

I started to get more orders for arrangements. Some people would give them as gifts. Others would use them as centerpieces for special occasions. The more orders I got, the more plants I bought.

Over time, I collected more than what our garden could hold. To accommodate my growing collection, and keep them organized, we built vertical gardens. Our once-bare patio became enclosed with ledges filled with succulents. I also have some of them planted in the ground, in containers, vertical frames, and hanging baskets. I even use repurposed items like old benches, chairs, and upside-down tables.

It was not easy in the beginning. Just like some of you who might have started and failed, I, too, had my share of failures and frustrations. But instead of giving up, I tried to learn whatever I could and find out what worked best. I would experiment and pay attention to even the littlest changes.

Being surrounded with a multitude of succulents, some of those with names I still do not know, has given me the opportunity to observe them every day. To learn more, I would visit our local library and bring home books about succulents. But the best things I've learned have come directly from working with these plants.

One day, it dawned on me that these plants, though unable to speak, communicate what is wrong with them. To understand, all we have to do is pay attention.

The best way to avoid frustration is to start this hobby right; that is, by investing your time to learn about what makes succulents so different from other plants, by finding out their greatest strengths and using it to your advantage. Be aware of their weaknesses, so that deadly mistakes can be avoided.

When I finally figured out the best way to take care of succulents, I decided to share my plants and the lessons I have learned with others.

Mission San Luis Rey
Oceanside, California

MY FIRST
FOUNTAIN
ARRANGEMENT

I was able to turn my passion into an income-generating hobby by selling succulent arrangements and cuttings. *Chopstick and Succulents* YouTube channel was born and has guided thousands of succulent newbies on how to keep their plants alive.

There are tricks I've found very useful and have guided me to success. Those tricks are what I am going to share with you in this book. I hope you'll find inspiration and reap the benefits this succulent hobby brings.

No more guessing. Know what you are doing and why. No more trial and error. I did that for you already. No more wasting your succulents. It's time to multiply them.

A
GARDEN
IS
A
FRIEND
YOU
CAN
VISIT
ANYTIME

Chopstick and Succulents

CHAPTER ONE

* START YOUR HOBBY RIGHT

* SUCCULENT PLANT'S IDENTIFICATION

Start Your Hobby Right

Nobody becomes an expert overnight—for sure not with succulents.

There are so many succulents to collect, from rosette-shaped Echeverias to stacked-leaved Crassulas. Some succulent plants are toxic, while others are edible. Most thrive better and are colorful in full sun, yet some will show their intricately-designed leaves when in low-light conditions.

You will need to know some things about the plants that you are growing so you can properly take care of them: how to water, light requirements, what temperatures they prefer and tolerate, and where they grow best.

If you are one of those with pets or small children, it is important to know which ones are safe to be around.

If growing these plants indoors is your intention, choosing the species that will thrive in such a location is what you might need to consider first.

If you live in places where it snows during the winter, growing frost-tolerant ones like Sempervivums and some cold-hardy Sedums might be your best choice. Unless, you are willing to invest in some grow lights and transfer your plants indoors when the temperature drops.

Most of us are new to this kind of plant. To learn, we often search online for tips.

As you search for more information about the care of your plants, you will notice that they have different groupings.

All living organisms are classified into different groups with varying degrees of relatedness. In the plant kingdom, these levels of classification include class, order, family, genus, and species.

Yes, your beloved succulent belongs to a family.

Plants that have something in common are grouped as family. They either have similar blooms, reproductive structures, or other similar characteristics. Knowing which family a plant belongs to can help you narrow down your search for their identification.

The family they are a member of can also give you an idea of how the plants' flowers may look. For example, plants that are members of the Asteraceae family are flowering plants, and their blooms look like daisies.

It can also help you identify which plants are toxic. For example, the common characteristics among plants belonging to the Euphorbiaceae family is the presence of the milky-white latex that bleeds out from the plant when cut. This sap is toxic.

Or you can tell how efficient they are at handling water. Like those that belong to the Crassulaceae family utilizes a special type of photosynthesis called CAM (or crassulacean acid metabolism), which allows the plants of this group to conserve water effectively by opening their stomata at night when it is cooler and closing them during the day when it is hot.

You will know they are referring to a plant's family when the word starts with a capital letter and often ends in ceae, like in Crassulaceae, Cactaceae, Liliaceae, Euphorbiaceae, and many more.

The Genus And Species

Each plant has a botanical name that is recognized by gardeners, horticulturists, and botanists around the world. It is made up of two parts, a genus (generic name) and species (specific name). It is always written with the generic name first, that begins with a capital letter, followed by the species, written in lower-case letters.

For example, Portulacaria afra, Aloe vera, Sedum morganianum, Aeonium arboreum...

Portulacaria afra
'Elephant Bush'

Euphorbia trigona
'Rubra'

Aeonium arboreum
'Zwartkop'

Aloe vera

Crassula perforata
'String of Buttons'

Echeveria gibbiflora
'Ruffled'

Graptoveria paraguayense
'Ghost Plant'

Sedum adolphii
'Golden Sedum'

Portulacaria afra
'Variegata'

Crassula tetragona
'Miniature Pine Tree'

Crassula ovata
'Tricolor'

Aloe vera

The genus (plural genera) is a collective name for the group of plants that share some similar characteristics or are classified based on their features. Their similarity may or may not be obvious.

The term genus comes from the Latin *genus*, meaning *origin, type, group, or race*.

Genus names are often derived from mostly Latin or Greek words, as well as other languages, describing the characteristics of the plant or named after a notable person in their honor, or had contributed to make the plant known.

Echeveria- named after Atanasio Echeverria y Godoy, the Mexican botanical artist during the 18th century who drew images of succulent plants.

Euphorbia- derives from Euphorbos, the Greek Physician who wrote that one of the cactus-like Euphorbias was used as a laxative.

Latin was the language that most educated people knew in the 18th century. It is the international language used by scientists to name plants.

While the species often (but not always) describes some characteristics of the plant, their specific name distinguishes different plants within a genus. Species names can be descriptive of the plants' color, the shape of the leaves or flowers, or where the plant grows.

For example:
Their color; rubra (red), padilla (cream), alba (white). Their shape; compacta (compact), longifolia (with long leaves), longiflora (with long flowers). Where they grow; Capensis (from the Cape, South Africa), rupestris (of hills).

Succulent Plants
IDENTIFICATION

Succulents are a group of plants defined by their heightened ability to store water. It is this ability that is responsible for their unique appearance and behavior, both of which sets them apart from more traditional houseplants. But contrary to popular belief, the term "succulent" does not apply to a family of plants in a biological sense, as succulents represent a broad array of unrelated plant species.

The word "succulent" derives from the Latin word sucus, which means juice, sap, or moisture. There-in lies the most important distinguishing characteristic of this unique cohort of plants. To put it simply, it's the way they handle water.

Plants need water for survival. But most utilize only a small percentage of what the roots take in. They lose about 97 to 99.5 percent of water by transpira-tion, a process where plants take up water through the roots and release water vapor through pores.

Plants need water to convert energy from sunlight into food through photosynthesis. They also need water for turgidity.

You see, plants do not have bones. Water makes up their skeleton. They need the right amount of pressure inside their cells to keep them upright. Not having enough water produces less force inside their leaves, making them limp.

However, succulent plants are different. They can hold moisture inside their cells and keep it from escaping, which means they can withstand dry conditions or prolonged dry spells.

Succulents detect water shortages and have techniques to conserve their supply to survive. The defensive strategies a succulent uses depend on its genes. In a drought, it's these genes that determine a succulent's ability to survive.

Nowadays, succulents are trendy. They are being sold all over the place; online, in local nurseries, and in garden centers. With so much access to succulents, we can easily buy them without knowing much about their care. Then, we might give them water more often than they need and wonder why they die.

Succulents are categorized into different genera. *Echeveria, Haworthia, Sedum, Euphorbia, Kalanchoe, Aeonium, Agave, Aloe, Crassula, Sempervivum* are among them. But there are so many more.

Within each genus are the species and varieties. Some of them are hybrids, and the list keeps on growing.

Let's briefly discuss their interesting characteristics per genera, and hopefully you can decide which ones you are interested to grow and collect.

Not all of them are included in this book. Most of the succulents that I am familiar with, and which I often use for my projects, are what you will see.

What's Interesting About
Aeonium

Pronounced ay-OH-nee-um.

A genus of about thirty-five species.
They belong to the Crassulaceae family.

Aside from containing all the vowels of the English alphabet in its name, *Aeonium* comes from the Greek word *aionos*, meaning *ageless* or *eternal*, because of its resilience.

They produce the most beautiful bloom. When trimmed together with some leaves, the flowers can last for more than a month in a vase without water.

The leaves are arranged in a rosette and come in a variety of colors. It can be from different shades of green to black. Some are multi-colored and bright, deserving the name of the brightest members of the solar system: the sun, moon, and stars! Have you seen the 'Sunburst,' 'Moonburst,' and 'Starburst'?

They bloom late winter or early spring and some are **monocarpic**. Each rosette **flowers only once** and **dies**. The plant uses all its energy to sustain the flowers and seeds..

But don't freak out because, before it dies, it will try to survive its race by producing a lot of offsets.

They have the **most delicate leaves**. Even with a slight touch, their leaves **can bruise**. They are not the ideal plants for projects that need frequent handling, like bouquets.

Aeoniums can grow like shrubs, or a single rosette may sit on a leggy stem.

They propagate from stem cuttings. You can snap a branch, allowing the tip to dry and heal in a warm and dry location, away from direct sunlight, for a few days and then plant in the soil.

Although their leaves are fleshy, they are not as plump compared to other succulent plants. One of the reasons why propagating them from leaves does not produce much success. That is true, especially to those flat-leaved varieties, as they tend to dry out and couldn't sustain a new life.

Their growing season is during winter to spring when temperatures are milder. They go dormant in summer and may close up their leaves like a tightly-closed rosette. When the climate becomes cooler, they come out of dormancy, and the rosettes open up again.

Full sun to part shade is what they prefer. Although in extreme heat, their leaves curl up and can get sunburned. But when exposed continuously to full sun, some can withstand once adjusted. With the abundance of light, their variegated counterparts show off amazing colors.

They do best in temperatures between 40 and 90 degrees Fahrenheit.

Aeoniums are not toxic to pets and humans.

AEONIUMS

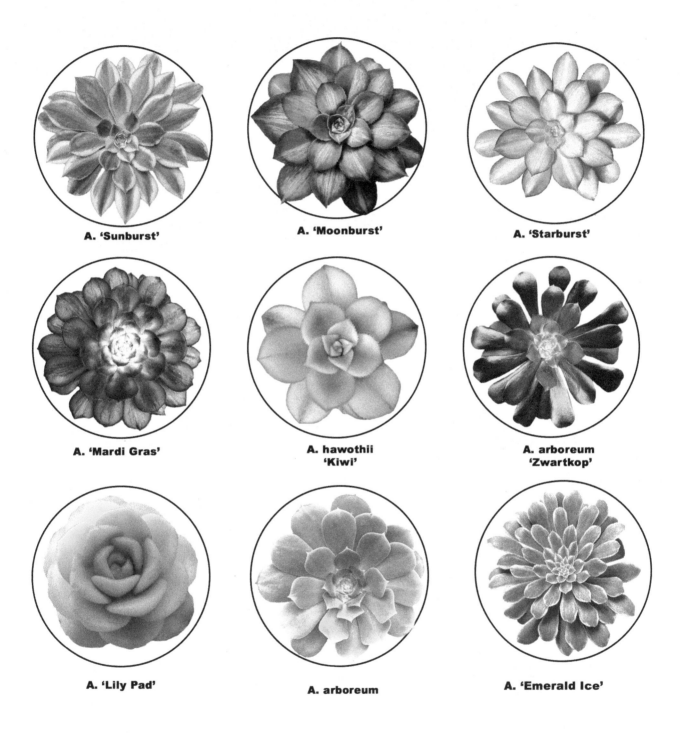

A. 'Sunburst'

A. 'Moonburst'

A. 'Starburst'

A. 'Mardi Gras'

A. hawothii
'Kiwi'

A. arboreum
'Zwartkop'

A. 'Lily Pad'

A. arboreum

A. 'Emerald Ice'

What You Need To Know About Echeveria

Pronounced ECH-i-VEER-ee-uh.

This plant is named after Atanasio Echeverria y Godoy, the 18th-century Mexican botanical illustrator.

As a member of the Crassulaceae family, they are drought-tolerant plants. Their leaves are not only fleshy, they also photosynthesize in a special way.

These rosette-shaped succulents are very popular as ornamental plants. With their attractive colors, unique shapes, and textures, it's hard not to fall for their alluring beauty.

Perhaps their striking appearance has to do with the arrangement of their leaves. They radiate from the center stalk and mostly grow close to the ground. Their fleshy leaves and compact rosettes look like flowers. Some look like giant, colorful cabbage.

They are beautiful displayed on their own or mixed with other succulent species in an arrangement, but unlike cut flowers that are short-lived, they can last for years and even produce more when cared for properly.

They are **polycarpic**, meaning they **can flower** and **set seeds many times over** the course of their lifetime.

They can also produce offsets, and are commonly called *hen and chicks*, where the hen is the mother plant and the chicks are the small babies surrounding it.

To maintain their compact shape and bright colors, they need abundant sunlight, proper watering, and the right conditions. Although they need full sun to maintain their vibrant colors, too much heat without allowing them time to adjust can damage their delicate leaves, too.

They are easy to cross-breed by pollinating one variety with another. There are such a large number of hybrids available in the market that it is sometimes hard to identify them. Some have bumps, others have frills and curls, and most have astonishing colors.

They are safe for pets and children.

Although growing them from seeds may take longer, it is pretty rewarding.

They prefer average to low humidity (40–50% or lower). The ideal temperature for these tender succulents is between 50 and 70 degrees Fahrenheit.

They are so easy to care for, as they can tolerate a bit of neglect when it comes to watering.

ECHEVERIAS

E. 'Perl Von
Nurnberg'

E. 'Mahogany Rose'

E. colorata

E. gibbiflora

E. 'Chroma'

E. 'Cubic Frost'

E. setosa
var. oteroi

E. 'Atlantis'

E. 'Violet Queen'

ECHEVERIAS

E. multicaulis
'Copper Rose'

E. minima

E. lilacina
'Ghost Echeveria'

E. gibbiflora
var. carunculata

E. Yamatoren

E. purpusorum

E. 'Lola'

E. 'Dusty Rose'

E. runyonii
'Topsy Turvy'

ECHEVERIAS

E. 'Doris Taylor'

E. 'Black Prince'

E. agavoides
'Lipstick'

E. 'Blue Atoll'

E. 'Raindrops'

E. 'Afterglow'

E. nodulosa
'Painted Echeveria'

E. pulidonis

E. 'Licorice'

Say Hello To
Aloe

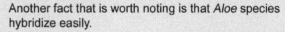
Aloe vera

Pronounced al-oh.

From the family of Asphodelaceae. They are flowering plants with a wide scattered distribution. They are often grown for ornamental and medicinal reasons.

Perhaps the most noted among this species is the *Aloe vera*. It has been applied for centuries as an alternative remedy. The earliest report of its use by humans is tracked back to the 16th century. Ancient Greeks and Romans used them to treat wounds.

A lot of products containing *Aloe vera* are available in the market. From skin-care products such as makeup, moisturizers, and sunscreen to juice drinks.

But out of the over 500 species of *Aloes*, only a few are used as traditional medicine.

Aloes are flowering plants with succulent leaves. They bloom early winter to spring, and their tubular flowers are either yellow, pink, orange, or red.

Most Aloes grow at the ground level. Some can become huge; others are low-growing, and form a thick mat.

They can be grown indoors or outdoors, in pots, or used for landscapes.

Aloe vera

Another fact that is worth noting is that *Aloe* species hybridize easily.

Combining two *Aloes* through cross-pollination results in a hybrid.

There are naturally occurring hybrids where the native pollinators are birds, bees, or butterflies. They can carry the pollen from the plant to different species that are compatible.Although naturally occurring hybrids oftentimes exist in nature, most of the hybrids we find in the market today results from human intervention.

Hybridizers often develop a better version of the species used—a more colorful version, with improved appeal through their leaf patterns resulting in much prettier and more resilient plants. Many hybrids are a small size that is perfect for container gardens. There are variegated varieties with exciting color combinations.

There are so many *Aloe* hybrids coming out in the market nowadays. Their numbers are growing at such a fast pace that keeping up with their names becomes a challenge. Some even look so alike that it's hard to tell them apart.

Some are miniatures and are great for containers.

They thrive best in temperatures between 50 and 85 degrees Fahrenheit.

Aloe vera is known for its medical uses, and using topical *Aloe vera* products does not have significant side effects. Oral ingestion of some *Aloe vera*, however, can be mildly toxic. When ingested, it can cause abdominal upset like vomiting and diarrhea. It is because some *Aloe* species contain a compound called *Aloin*, which has a laxative effect.

Aloe
arborescens

Euphorbia tirucalli 'Firesticks'
Crassula ovata 'Gullom' Jade
Crassula ovata 'Hummel's Sunset'
Portulacaria afra f. variegata
Aloe cameronii 'Starfish Aloe'

ALOES

A. aborescens f. variegata

A. 'Pink Blush'

A. 'White Beauty'

Aloiampelos ciliaris

A.'Blizzard'

A. juvenna 'Tiger Tooth'

A.'Christmas Carol'

A. polyphylla 'Spiral Aloe'

A. brevifolia 'Crocodile Plant'

What's To Love About
Haworthias

Haworthia fasciata
'Zebra Plant'

Pronounced haw-wur-thee-uh.

Most *Haworthias* are small and are slow-growers. They are the ideal plants for container gardens and those with limited space.

Aside from being small and convenient, they are more tolerant of low-light conditions. Compared to other succulents, they can thrive well indoors.

The unique shapes, textures, and unusual patterns on their leaves inspire collectors. Some *Haworthias* are low-growing rosettes. Others have chunky translucent leaves designed to store more water.

Haworthia is named after the English entomologist, botanist, and carcinologist, Adrian Hardy Haworth.

Some *Haworthias* are sometimes confused with *Aloes*. The *Haworthia fasciata* is one great example. It's understandable because they belong to the same Asphodelaceae family. But unlike *Aloes*, *Haworthias* are small and slow-growing.

Some *Haworthias* have delicate fleshy leaves with translucent windows, which are great for terrariums and miniature landscapes with low-light requirements.

Most succulents propagate faster through leaves and cuttings. But *Haworthias* are good at producing a lot of offsets. It may take up to one year or more for a small plant to grow them, but it's worth the wait.

You can leave the babies to grow around their mother to form a clump, or you can separate them and propagate more. When separating the offsets from the mother plant, allow them to callus for a day or two before planting them in the soil.

The best time for propagation is springtime. When you happen to uproot, you will notice that some *Haworthias* have roots that are longer than the plant that is visible on top of the soil. Some are fleshier.

They can tolerate underwatering, but can rot when overwatered.

Add pebbles or small rocks on top of the soil when planting in containers. The top dressings will not only improve their presentation, but will also prevent plants from sitting on wet ground.

They prefer moderate light. Bright but indirect sunlight is best.

Some *Haworthias*, when placed in the shade, may lose their compact shape. But when exposed to direct sunlight, however, those with thin translucent leaves can easily scorch. Therefore, they are not the kind of plants you want exposed to full sun to become colorful.

They are not poisonous to humans and animals.

Not cold hardy. They do best in temperatures between 50 and 90 degrees Fahrenheit.

Haworthia fasciata
'Zebra Plant'

HAWORTHIAS

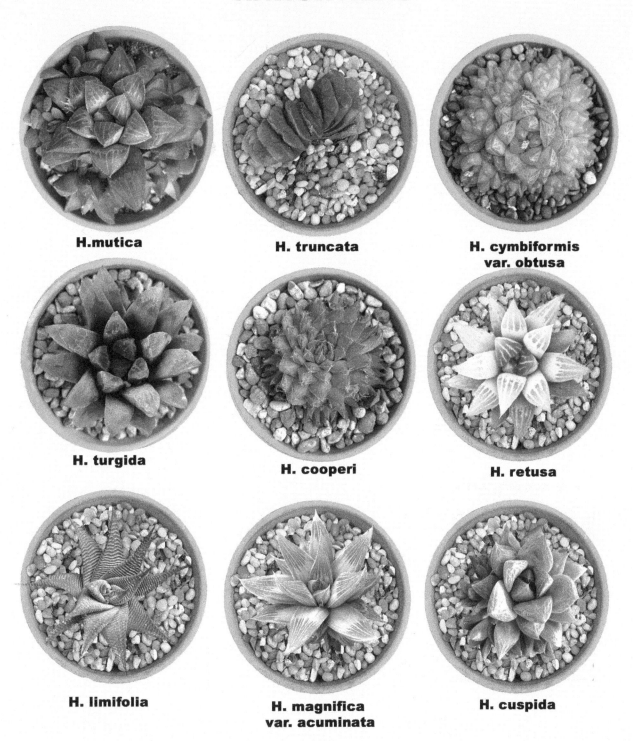

H.mutica

H. truncata

H. cymbiformis
var. obtusa

H. turgida

H. cooperi

H. retusa

H. limifolia

H. magnifica
var. acuminata

H. cuspida

Theresa Jimeno Ebro

why Euphorbia
Should Be Handled With Care

Pronounced yoo-fawr-bee-uh.

These plants come from the Euphorbiaceae family, called *"spurge"* from the Middle English *espurge*, meaning to *purge*. It is because the sap of the plant is used as purgative. The botanical name *Euphorbia* is named after a Greek physician, Euphorbos, who wrote that cactus-like *Euphorbia (Euphorbia obtusifolia ssp. regis-jubae)* is a powerful laxative.

The typical attribute among *Euphorbia* is the viscous, milky-white latex bleeding out from the plant when cut. It is toxic. The sap that leaks out even with the smallest cut is the plants' way of defending themselves from herbivores who can feed on them in the wild.

It can irritate the skin to a varying degree, depending on how sensitive an individual is. A slight drop of latex can irritate the skin. It will hurt even more if it goes in your eyes. It can cause serious damage, even temporary blindness.

Euphorbia tirucalli 'Fire Sticks,' for example, may look harmless, but be wary when dealing with the plant. Always wear gloves and eye protection when clipping.

People often mistook *Euphorbias* for cacti. Aside from the fact that some *Euphorbias* are sometimes mislabeled as cacti, they also look like them. They are not at all related because *Euphorbia* belongs to the Euphorbiaceae family, while cacti belongs to the Cactaceae family.

But there's what they call convergent evolution, wherein species from different lineages living in the same challenging location evolved and developed the same features or traits to solve the same problems. In the case of both cacti and *Euphorbias*, it's the challenge of surviving in arid locations as well as protecting their stored water supply.

Here are a few distinctions that can aid you in identifying them:

*Euphorbias secrete sticky-milky sap when cut; cacti do not.

*Some *Euphorbias* have thorns that grow out from their stem, while cacti have spines that are modified leaves growing out from their areoles.

*Euphorbia flowers are discreet, while cacti have gorgeous showy flowers.

Euphorbia blossoms are not as attractive compared to other succulent plants, but their charm rests in their extraordinary shape and form.

On the favorable side, *Euphorbias* are simple to cultivate. Once established, they require minimal upkeep. They can flourish in ordinary soil conditions as long as they are not constantly wet.

They do well in bright, direct sunlight and thrive better in temperatures between 55 and 80 degrees Fahrenheit.

Euphorbia flanaganii 'Medusa's Head'

EUPHORBIAS

E. leucadendron

E. trigona
'Rubra'

E. ledienii

E. tirucalli
'Sticks on Fire'

E. mammillaris
f. variegata

E. obesa
'Basketball Plant'

E. flanaganii
'Medusa's Head'

E. anoplia
'Tanzanian Zipper Plant'

E. milii
'Crown of Thorns'

Theresa Jimeno Ebro

Kalanchoe

You'll Either Love Them Or Not!

Kalanchoe blossfeldiana

Pronounced kal-uh n-koh-ee, kuh-lan-choh.

Kalanchoe is a genus of about 125 species and belongs to the Crassulaceae family—a diverse group of blossoming plants. They have leaves that are succulent and use a special form of photosynthesis: CAM, crassulacean acid metabolism.

The name *Kalanchoe* came from the Chinese name *Kalan Chauhuy*, which means *that which falls and grows.*

This group consists of plants with splendid flowers, but, at the same time, are some of the most troublesome weeds among succulent plants.

Kalanchoe tubiflora 'Mother of Millions' and *Kalanchoe delagoensis* 'Mother of Thousands,' for example, are not only toxic, but highly invasive. One of their interesting features is the tiny plantlets growing along the edges of their leaves called bulbils. They are clones of the mother plant that can grow once dropped on the ground.

Though they have the most gorgeous and lasting flowers, they are unwanted in some parts of the world and are classified as invasive weeds. Both plants contain Bufadienolides, a cardiac glycoside that can lead to cardiac arrest in animals once consumed in a substantial amount.

The same toxic plants have been subject to several studies because of their anti-tumor-promoting effects and insecticide properties. It's fascinating how this plant can be dangerous yet helpful at the same time.

They are grown as ornamental house plants and do great for rock gardens and landscapes—well-loved for their low upkeep and drought tolerance.

They prefer full sunlight exposure and can stand a minor extent of frost.

If you are considering a low-maintenance house plant with colorful flowers, *Kalanchoe blossfeldiana* is the best choice for you. Their bloom lasts longer and helps purify the air indoors, too.

To enjoy them indoors, locate that sunniest spot, place in a well-ventilated area, and protect them from drafts. Do not put them inside your bathroom.

Kalanchoe was one of the first plants sent to the moon. They grow best in temperatures between 45 and 85 degrees Fahrenheit.

Kalanchoe laetivirens bulbils

KALANCHOES

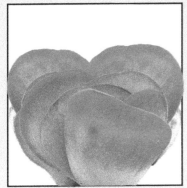

K. luciae
'Flapjack'

K. beharensis
'Velvet Elephant Ear'

K. tomentosa
'Chocolate Soldier'

K. fedtschenkoi
'Lavender Scallops'

K. eriophylla
'Snow White Panda'

K. humilis

K. tubiflora
'Mother of Millions'

K. delagoensis
'Pink Mother of Thousands'

K. tomentosa
'Panda Plant'

Why Beginners Should Try
Crassula

Crassula perforata f. variegata'
'String of Buttons'

Pronounced KRAS-ew-la.

They are the simplest plants to grow in the garden. The kind that, when stable, will not demand considerable attention. When watered and placed in the shade, they will become green and may look like common plants, but once cut down and left unplanted for a month without soil or water, they will show how tough they are.

The name *Crassula* comes from the Latin *crassus*, meaning *thick*. It is a genus of succulent plants having about 350 species. They are members of the Crassulaceae family and exist in many parts of the world.

They can also grow and resemble tiny mature trees like bonsai, but some can become thick like shrubs. Some *Crassula* species have stacked leaves that develop on top of each other. But some varieties are miniature, like the *Crassula rupestris* 'Tom Thumb' that can be as small as a baby's pinky finger. Some can grow upright or spill out from their containers. They are best planted in hanging baskets or mixed with other succulents in an arrangement.

They blossom in spring and summer. Some have beautiful flowers, while others are trivial. Trimming the spent flowers can promote healthy new growth.

They require bright light to bring about their most vibrant colors. Once adapted to the heat of the sun, they are resilient even during the hottest part of summer. Certain *Crassula* varieties can tolerate a dingy box for a month without wilting, lengthening, or changing color. I noticed that, when one pack of cuttings I sold returned to me unclaimed after over thirty days, while some succulents inside the package turned pale and twisted, *Crassula ovata* 'Gullom' stood the same.

If you are contemplating a low-maintenance plant that you can grow either indoors or outdoors, try *Crassula ovata*. They are excellent at surviving in conditions with restricted water.

Once stable, these plants are capable of self-care and are tough. They are resilient to pests, continued drought, the intense heat of the sun, and even occasional frost.

They can get through the tests of Mother Nature, but no matter how massive and stable the plants are, the roots and stems will decay when left sitting in water for a lengthy period.

They are mildly toxic to children and pets and are at their best at temperatures between 40 and 90 degrees Fahrenheit.

Crassula perforata f. variegata'
'String of Buttons'

CRASSULAS

C. ovata
'Hobbit'

C. ovata
'Tricolor'

C. perforata f. variegata
'String of Buttons'

C. rubricaulis

C. congesta

C. arborescens
'Ripple Jade'

C. capitella
'Campfire'

C. rupestris
'Baby Necklace'

C. capitella
ssp. thyrsiflora

Theresa Jimeno Ebro

Sedum—
Some are cold-hardy; some are not.

Pronounced see-duhm.

Sedum is a large genus of flowering plants in the Crassulaceae family. They are commonly known as stonecrops. They are about 500 species of plants with water-storing leaves and stems.

These plants are very easy to grow and multiply. They are great for novices, as they do not call for extraordinary skills to grow. They will grow even in poor soil as long as it drains out easily. They are not merely attractive; they are rather hardy as well.

Sedum species vary in their needs; some are cold-hardy but do not endure prolonged heat; some can endure heat but cannot tolerate cold.

Those with chunky leaves can survive prolonged heat and drought because of their stored water, while those creeping ones with thinner leaves will turn crisp and dry when exposed to prolonged drought without watering well.

Some *Sedums* are edible.

There are two groups of *Sedums*, the upright-growing, and the creeping ones. Both are excellent for containers. The tall ones would look great in any pots, and the creeping types will do well in hanging baskets and spillers for arrangements.

The creeping *Sedums* are good as ground covers. They are low-spreading and reaching only a few inches above the ground. Their foliage is colorful and even comes in various shades. Although creeping, they are non-invasive. With their shallow roots, it's easy to take them out when required. Some of these creeping *Sedums* are frost-tolerant.

The tall and upright-growing *Sedums* have fleshy leaves and store water in their chunky leaves and stems. They do well in the vertical garden.

Propagating them from leaves is easy. They can snap from the parent stem with less effort, ensuring an intact meristem. If you want to try propagating from leaves, these chunky *Sedums* are the best to use. The best time to plant them is in early spring after the threat of frost is over, and the heat is not yet intense.

Sedum spurium 'Red Carpet'

Sedum spurium 'Tricolor'

SEDUMS

**S. adolphii
Sedum nussbaumerianum"**

**S. adolphii
'Firestorm'**

**S. adolphii
'Golden Glow'**

**S. pachyphyllum
'Salsa'**

**S. dendroideum
Tree Stonecrop'**

**S. rubrotinctum
'Jelly Bean'**

**S. rubrotinctum
'Aurora'
'Pink Jelly Bean'**

**S. morganianum
'Burro's Tail'**

S. clavatum

Did You Know That Not All **Senecios** *Are Succulents?*

Pronounced suh-nee-see-ow.

Senecio is one of the broadest genera of flowering plants. Out of more than 1,250 species of *Senecios*, about a hundred of them are succulents. They are a genus of the daisy family (Asteraceae).

The name *Senecio* means old man.

Some *Senecio* species have toxic fluids to discourage or kill creatures that would devour them. So, plant them with caution. Keep them out of reach if you have pets or young children.

Some grow like shrubs, others remain small and are excellent for ground covers, yet others are trailing down and best grown in hanging baskets. They look splendid with their stems dangling.

Those with trailing stems usually have common names describing the form of each leaf. The 'String of Pearls' *(Senecio rowleyanus)*, 'String of Bananas' *(Senecio radicans)*, and 'String of Dolphins' *(Senecio peregrinus)* are just a few examples.

Trailing *Senecios* do well in bright shade, but most shrubs and groundcovers do well in full sun.

They can withstand short periods of dampness and cold temperatures, but prolonged exposure can damage them. So, avoid letting them sit on wet soil to prevent rot. When well established, they are drought-tolerant and heat-tolerant and can withstand a bit of neglect.

They are dormant during the winter, and it is best to keep their soil dry during this period.

Senecio rowleyanus
'String of Pearls'

Senecio radicans
'String of Bananas'

Senecio peregrinus
'String of Dolphins'

SENECIOS

S. barbetonicus

S. crassisimus

**S. haworthii
'Cocoon Plant'**

**S. mandraliscae
'Blue Chalks'**

**S. jacobsenii
'Trailing Jade'**

**S. longiflorus
'Paintbrush Flower'**

**S. kleiniiformis
'Spear Head'**

**S. stapeliiformis
'Pickle Plant'**

**S. herreianus
'String of Watermelon'**

Cold-Hardy Sempervivums

Pronounced sem-per-vahy-vuhm.

Sempervivums belongs to the Crassulaceae family. These plants are harmless around pets and children, as they are not toxic.

Although further evidence is required to evaluate its efficiency, this plant is utilized to treat certain conditions. The juice from its leaves is used to manage acute diarrhea. It has no known serious side effects, but it can induce vomiting when consumed in considerable quantities. It can likewise help in problems of swelling due to water retention.

The extract from its leaves was utilized in folk remedies for centuries. The slightly warmed juice from its leaves blended with honey can help soothe aches from mouth lesions; crushed leaves can be applied topically to treat boils and heal wounds; it can likewise be applied to stop nose bleeding.

The leaves, when macerated and infused with vinegar, can be used to get rid of warts and corns. Just like *Aloe vera*, the leaf pulp is used to make cooling face masks for sunburned or reddened skin and insect bites.

The name *Sempervivum* comes from the Latin *semper*, meaning *always*, and *vivum*, meaning *living* because the plant continues living and retains its leaves in winter and is resilient to stressful conditions. Another name for *Sempervivum* is houseleeks. It is thought to come from the old practices in some places in Europe of cultivating plants on roofs to ward off fires and lightning. Welsh people have a traditional folk belief that having these plants cultivated on the roof provides the health and wealth of those who live there.

The particular interest in this plant is not the flowers, but how the petals are arranged. They develop a compact flock of low-growing rosettes that can form a mat.

Sempervivums earned the name hens and chicks from the manner in which they grow offsets. When conditions are favorable, they proliferate rapidly via offsets. These baby plants can be snapped off and replanted individually. Each rosette (a hen) propagates offsets growing around it like chicks. Just like *Aeonium*, *Sempervivums* are also monocarpic. After several years, possibly between two and five years, the parent plant will yield a flower stalk with small star-shaped flowers. Then the mother plant (a hen) will perish, but the offsets (chicks) will go on living.

They can withstand hostile conditions like locations with restricted access to water. This makes them great for vertical projects and rock gardens. They are remarkably resistant to cold and can even survive deep freezes.

Be Creative
With Succulents

Sempervivums
'Purple Passion'

Fun Facts About
Portulacaria

Pronounced por-tew-luh-KAR-ee-uh.

The leaves are edible and can be used for soups and salads. They have a tart flavor and are high in Vitamin C. In South Africa, they serve as food for elephants. No wonder they are also called elephant bush.

Portulacaria afra is also called other names, such as 'Porkbush,' 'Spekboom,' or 'Elephant's Food,' and belong to the Didiereaceae family. The name *Portulacaria* is composed of *Portulaca* and aria, which suggest similar to *Portulaca*, and afra, referring to Africa.

Although sometimes called 'Dwarf Jade' or 'Miniature Jade,' they are not related at all to jade plants (*Crassula ovata*).

Aside from being edible, *Portulacaria* afra has so many uses. It can increase breast-milk production when eaten by lactating mothers. Sucking the juice from its leaves can treat exhaustion and quench thirst. The leaves, when crushed, can offer healing of blisters and corns on the feet. When chewed, it can treat sore throat and mouth infections. It can also offer relief from sunburn, pimples, rashes, and insect bites.

Most important of all, this plant is very helpful to our environment. Research has shown that this plant is an excellent 'carbon sponge.' It is more efficient in cleaning the air than other plants. It has the ability to absorb carbon dioxide from the environment effectively.

Portulacaria afra

Portulacaria afra 'Minima'

Portulacaria afra 'Variegata'

Portulacaria afra 'Medio-Picta'

Portulacaria afra 'Variegata

Sedum dendroideum

Portulacaria afra is drought-tolerant and can survive prolonged drought by utilizing special types of metabolism. Studies have shown that *Portulacaria afra* is a facultative CAM species. What this means is that it can perform daytime photosynthesis like other plants when conditions are favorable. But during times where water is limited, while other plants have to shut down to survive until the next rain comes, *Portulacaria afra* utilizes CAM photosynthesis and can continue to grow and survive during drought.

The plant can grow like shrubs in an upright manner or spread out laterally, and can also be grown into bonsai.

Portulacaria afra are sun-loving plants and perform best under warm conditions. They grow best at night-time temperatures between 55 and 65 degrees Fahrenheit and daytime temperatures between 80 and 90 degrees Fahrenheit.

Let **Sansevieria** *Bring You Luck*

Pronounced san-suh-vee-eer-ee-uh.

Sansevieria belongs to the Asparagaceae family. A genus of about seventy species, they are native to India, Indonesia, and Africa.

Sansevieria has various common names in different locations. They are commonly called 'Snake Plants' or 'Mother-in-law's Tongue' or 'Saint George's Sword' because of the shape and margins of their leaves.

They are also called 'Good Luck Plants.' In Barbados, they are referred to as 'Money Plant,' because of their belief that the individual possessing it will consistently have money.

They are also known as 'Viper's Bowstring Hemp' because they are one of the sources for plant fiber needed to make bowstrings. Fibers from this plant make solid threads, making them famous for making slingshots—a hand-powered projectile weapon.

They're a popular houseplant due to their low-light requirements. They thrive well in both bright-light locations as well as in shady corners.

They are great for the bedroom. When placed indoors, the plant can help reduce stress and clean the air by removing toxins. Although, their leaves are potentially toxic when ingested.

Named for Raimondo di Sangro, Prince of Sanseviero, an Italian scientist and inventor.

They can be propagated from seeds, leaf cuttings, and division. Propagating from seeds is rarely used because the other options are way faster.

When the shoot of *Sansevieria* blooms, it will stop producing new leaves but will continue to grow by producing plantlets from its creeping rootstocks. They can tolerate drought but will rot and die when left sitting in too much water. Therefore, fast-draining soil is essential, as well as a container with a hole.

Over time, they can get crowded in one pot and may need repotting.

They thrive best in temperatures between 55 and 85 degrees Fahrenheit.

Sansevieria trifasciata

SANSEVIERIAS

**S. cylindrica
'Starfish'**

**S. trifasciata
'Black Gold'**

**S. hahnii
'Birds Nest'**

**S. trifasciata
'Laurentii'**

**S. ehrenbergii
'Samurai'**

**S. suffruticosa
'Frosty Spears'**

GRAPTOPETALUM
The Best In Leaf Propagation

Graptopetalum is a small genus of about nineteen species belonging to the Crassulaceae family. The name comes from the Greek word *graptos*, meaning *marked* or *inscribed*, and *petalon*, meaning *petals*.

The most common species we see is the *Graptopetalum paraguayense*, commonly known as 'Ghost Plant,' or 'Mother of Pearl Plant'. You most probably are also familiar with the *Graptopetalum superbum*, which has smooth and flatter purplish-grey leaves.

They are the easiest succulents to propagate from leaves and cuttings. One can have a single cutting of this plant and end up multiplying them with less effort. Their chunky leaves can snap out effortlessly from the stem with a slight nudge, which often ensures an intact meristem. The rosette that breaks off can easily grow roots.

Both species enjoy full sun to partial sun. The intensity of their colors depend on the amount of sunlight received. When in the shade, they can have a pale bluish-green color with some tinge of purple, but when in full sun, the purple leaves get richer and can turn pink. Therefore, the same plant growing just a few feet away in the same garden may look different.

When planted in a container, it has the tendency to trail down. Usually with a single rosette at the end of a leggy stem.

Provide its basic growing needs—well-draining soil, sunlight, and water—and it will reward you with beautiful, colorful rosette-forming leaves with very little effort on your end.

This plant is not toxic to cats or dogs.

They can also hybridize with other genera:

Graptoveria= Graptopetalum x Echeveria
Examples are: *Graptoveria Debbie, G. Fred Ives, G. Bashful*

Graptosedum= Graptopetalum x Sedum
Examples are: *Graptosedum Vera Higgins, G. Darley Sunshine, G. California Sunset*

Graptopetalum amethystinum

Graptopetalum 'Superbum'

Intergenetic Hybrids

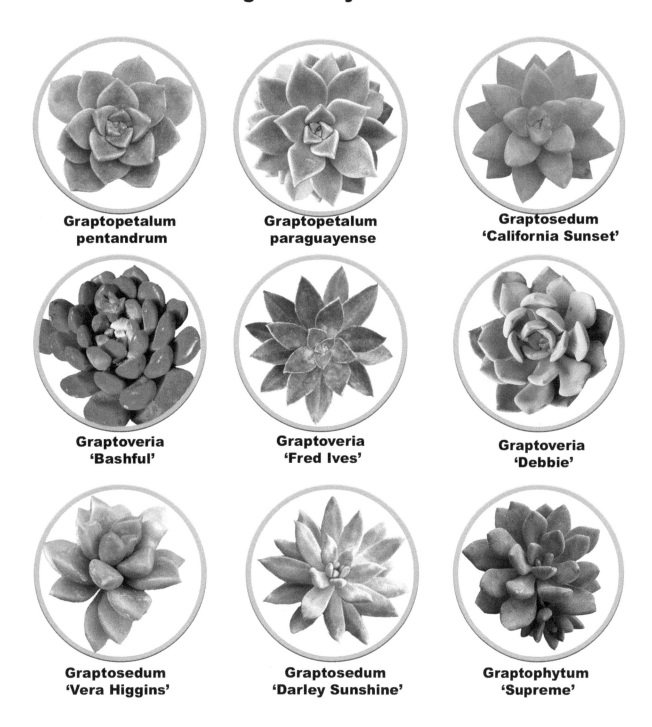

Graptopetalum
pentandrum

Graptopetalum
paraguayense

Graptosedum
'California Sunset'

Graptoveria
'Bashful'

Graptoveria
'Fred Ives'

Graptoveria
'Debbie'

Graptosedum
'Vera Higgins'

Graptosedum
'Darley Sunshine'

Graptophytum
'Supreme'

Cacti Versus Succulents

Cactus (plural cacti) is a member of the Cactaceae family of about 1,750 known species.

The majority of cacti are stem succulents. They can survive unattended in the wild relying on Mother Nature for their water supply.

Their extensive shallow roots can readily absorb rainwater and store it in their fleshy stems.

Like most succulents plants, they utilize CAM photosynthesis to conserve water.

They have spines which are modified leaves. They provide protection from herbivores as well as from the heat of the sun. These spines also trap moisture near the surface, creating a moisture layer that further reduces moisture loss.

Cactus stems are often fluted or ribbed and can expand when filled with rainwater and shrink during drought.

They adapt well to dry locations and can handle neglect. Planting them in fast-draining soil is important. They must not sit on wet soil, as it can cause them to rot.

Cacti do best in temperatures between 45 and 85 degrees Fahrenheit.

All Cacti Are Succulents, But Not All Succulents Are Cacti.

The terms "cacti" and "succulents" are often used interchangeably.

Plants that store water are generally known as succulents. Since all cacti store water, they are all considered succulents. But not all succulents are cacti.

To belong to a cacti family, a plant must have specialized structures called areoles. These are what separates them from other plants. Areoles are the round, cushion-like structures that all cacti have. It's where their spines, flowers, or hair grows.

Those fleshy *Echeverias*, *Kalanchoes*, and *Crassulas* are succulents, but they are not cacti.

CHAPTER TWO

UNDERSTANDING THE UNIQUENESS OF SUCCULENTS

THEIR CLEVER SELF-DEFENSE TACTICS

THEIR DROUGHT-SURVIVAL STRATEGIES

Understanding The Uniqueness Of Succulents

Different plant species have different physical structures and ways to manage water. There are three main groups of plants divided by their water requirements: hydrophytes, mesophytes, and xerophytes.

Hydrophytes are plants that grow in water. Obviously, they need lots of water to survive. Simple enough.

Mesophytes are what we usually see on a day-to-day basis. These plants need an average amount of water. They grow and thrive in average conditions that are neither wet nor dry.

Xerophytes are plants adapted to dry locations. They live in areas with limited access to water, such as deserts or snow-covered regions in the Alps or Arctic. These plants need the least amount of water.

Cacti and succulents are xerophytes. They are common in the desert, where rain falls unpredictably. Their ability to store and conserve water is a huge factor in their survival.

But not all xerophytes are succulents, however. Remember, succulents are plants that store water. Some xerophytes do not hold water but survive drought by having small leaves. Some shed their leaves to preserve their species.

Other xerophytic plants become dormant and stop growing during periods of drought. Although some may look dead, they will come to life again when water is available.

The structures of these three types of plants differ, as do the chemical processes they use for survival.

Hydrophytes have thin, flat leaves with a multitude of open pores (stomata). Their roots are also shorter and less dense than plants in other categories. Mesophytes, like our common houseplants, have an average amount of stomata, or pores. Most of their pores are on the underside of their leaves. They also have well-developed root systems.

Xerophytes have deep, spreading roots, and some, such as cacti and succulents, can store water.

A plant's size and amount of pores influence the rate of water loss. The more pores, the more exit points for water to escape. The bigger the holes and the larger the surface area, the more pores present, which means more water escapes. The thicker the skin, the less water escapes.

The environment also contributes to water loss. Temperature, humidity, air movement, and light intensity all impact how much water escapes from a plant.

Their Life In The Wild

A plant's life in the desert is difficult because of the infrequent rainfall. On top of that, they need to deal with rapid fluctuations in daily temperatures. The sunlight can be strong during the day, but the nights can be very cold. Despite these harsh conditions, cacti and succulents can survive. That is because they have adapted to their environments and have ways to protect themselves.

In the desert, it is usually dry and very hot during the day. Temperatures exceeding one hundred degrees are not uncommon. At night, the same location can have temperatures below forty degrees. The structures of succulent plants are built to survive in places such as this.

Most of the succulent plants we bring to our home do not come from the wild. Most are grown indoors in greenhouses. Although grown outside their native habitat, they still possess the genes and structures of their species. Therefore, they are capable of protecting themselves.

Some of these plants make their own sunscreen, which protects them from the sun's harmful rays. But unlike the sunscreen humans use, which we can apply when needed, succulents require time to produce their natural sun protection. They need to be gradually introduced to sun exposure so they can build the defenses that will protect them from damage. They need time to respond and generate enough sunscreen to protect themselves. If they are not ready, they can get sunburn marks that will not go away.

Succulents' Clever Self-Defense Tactics

In the desert, succulent plants possess the most valuable commodity: **water.**

The competition among living things in the desert is fierce, and the imbalance of supply and demand can result in an invasion. Insects and animals are thirsty, too, and can threaten a succulent's treasured supply.

Because of their water storage capabilities, succulents' lives are always threatened. To survive, they utilize physical and chemical ways of protecting themselves not only from the burning heat of the sun but also from thirsty mammals.

They are rooted on the ground and have no means to run away from danger. They need to defend themselves while remaining fixed in one place.

To protect themselves physically, succulents have structures that can alter to prepare for battle. Their leaves, which roll into thorny spikes over time, become their first line of defense. Herbivores are at risk of being stabbed when they come too close. Their spikes are like pointed stakes guarding a medieval castle.

Sometimes small insects pass through more significant spikes, but succulents have smaller ones for additional protection.

Farina and waxy coatings not only protect succulents from the sun but also make their walls slippery. This creates a very challenging surface for insect enemies to climb or cling to.

Chemically, succulents protect themselves by leaking toxic fluids when wounded. Their whitish sap can burn the skin of their enemies or poison those who drink their juice.

Finally, some succulents have mastered the skill of hiding. Lithops, for example, camouflage themselves by blending in with their surroundings and burying themselves underground. The translucent window located on top of their leaves enables them to continue absorbing the energy from the sun for photosynthesis.

How clever is that? Because they cannot run away, they hide instead.

Most of the features of succulents that fascinate us are key to their self-defense strategies. These plants are very resilient and built to survive in harsh environments. And even if part of a succulent gets damaged, other parts will continue to live and even regenerate.

List of mimicry plants below:

Aloinopsis malherbei, Fenestraria aurantiaca, Lithops, Pleiospilos nelii, Aloinopsis luckhoffii, Titanopsis calcareum.

When Stressed,
Succulents Change Color

Echeveria 'Afterglow'

The Lotus Effect of Epicuticular Wax

Epicuticular wax is the powdery coating on the surface of a plant's cuticle. It decreases surface wetting and moisture loss. It's the plant's natural sunscreen, protecting them from getting sunburned. It also creates a slippery surface, making it difficult for insects to climb.

SUCCULENTS' DROUGHT-SURVIVAL STRATEGIES

Here are some of the unique strategies succulents have to survive harsh weather conditions:

Water Storage

Succulents' ability to store water is what sets them apart from other plants. Their thickened leaves and fleshy stems are where they store their supply. When there's no more water available in the soil, they survive by utilizing their water supply.

Assorted Succulent Cuttings

Thick, Waxy Cuticle

The cuticle is a thin protective layer covering the surface of plants. The structure of some succulent leaves are thicker than other plants. Some plants that thrive in hot conditions have an outer leaf covering that is several layers thick. It protects them from excessive water loss.

Sedum dendroideum

Kalanchoe tomentosa 'Panda Plant'

Tomentose Leaves

Leaves covered with wooly hairs are called tomentose leaves. This comes from the Latin word *tomentosus,* meaning *having a mass of rough hairs.* These tiny hairs act as wind-breakers, reducing airflow and therefore evapotranspiration. These tomentose coverings also help trap moisture and insulate succulents from the drying effects of the wind.

Echeveria colorata

Natural Sunscreen

Epicuticular wax, is the flour-like coating present on succulent leaves and stems. This wax is the natural sunscreen that protects them from getting sunburned. But this wax also has other purposes. It creates a slippery surface, making it difficult for insects to climb the plant. It also forms a barrier that helps reduce moisture loss. Be careful when handling these plants. You want to avoid removing these protective layers.

Crassula capitella 'Campfire'

They Work At Night

Most succulent plants have crassulacean acid metabolism (CAM). This type of metabolism allows plants to close their stomata during the day and open them at night. At night, it is cooler and more humid, so water loss during transpirationis significantly lower.

Crassula ovata 'Gollum' Jade

Fewer Pores

Stomata are tiny openings on the surface of a plant's leaves and stems. These pores are essential for photosynthesis. But, they are also places where water can escape. It is crucial for plants living in dry places to reduce transpiration to conserve water. Having fewer and smaller pores helps succulents reduce the rate of transpiration.

Crassula ,Baby's Necklace'

Stacked Leaves

Several Crassula species have leaves that are tightly stacked. The stems are in the middle, surrounded by the leaves that pile up on top of each other. This helps reduce water loss by reducing the surface area directly exposed to the sun.

Echeveria 'Violet Queen'

Rosette Shapes

Rosette-shaped succulents have leaves that radiate from the center stalk. This leaf formation allows succulents to better capture sunlight but also close and protect themselves when the heat is too much. Their thick, fleshy leaves store water, and they open up and expand when water is plenty. When water is scarce, they close up to sleep. Most of them grow at the ground level to capture moisture the moment it is present.

Euphorbia anoplia 'Zipper Plant'

Ribbed Structure

The Euphorbia anoplia 'Tanzanian Zipper Plant' has pleated leaves that work like an accordion. They expand when water is abundant and contract when its supply is getting depleted.

Hair Growth

The exciting feature of Cephalocereus senilis 'Old Man's Cactus,' is its hair-like covering. The silvery-white hairy cover looks like the grey hair of anolder man. Its light color reflects sunlight to prevent it from scorching, providing shade that keeps the area cooler. It also protects these cacti from frost.

Cephalocereus senilis 'Old man's Cactus'

Opuntia engelmannii

Leaves Reduced To Spines

Most cacti species lack real leaves but have spines. By reducing the area exposed to the air, these spines reduce water loss. These spines also provide shade, trap moisture, and slow down air movement around the plant. They also protect the plant from herbivores that can devour their water supply.

Sedum pachyphyllum 'Jelly Beans'

They Change Colors

When stressed, succulents change colors. They can turn red, orange, pink, yellow, or in the case here, a rainbow color. Color changes are influenced by the presence of pigments anthocyanins and carotenoids. These changes protect them from harsh environmental conditions, such as extreme heat and cold.

CHAPTER THREE

*YOUR NEWLY-PURCHASED SUCCULENT
MAY DIE OF TOO MUCH WATER

*WHAT TO DO WHEN YOU BRING HOME
SUCCULENT PLANTS

Your Newly Purchased Succulents May Die From Overwatering

Have you experienced bringing home a healthy looking succulent that died a few days later?

It is such a baffling and disheartening experience to start a hobby. But, this is pretty common not only with complete novices but even with those who had years of experience growing plants.

Buying a healthy-looking plant and watching it perish without you doing anything to it, is particularly puzzling. It may lead you to believe that you are not competent in taking care of these plants or that their care needs are incredibly complicated.

The fact is, it's not you who killed the plant, and growing succulents is not complicated.

Unfortunately, a lot of plants displayed in large indoor stores are often overwatered. We choose them because they look so charming and plump, without knowing that their water storage is about to burst.

They may look healthy, but their storage chambers are like time-bombs that can explode anytime.

It is typical for succulent plants to have drawn too much water during their stay inside the nursery.

This scenario is notably typical in larger home supply retailers. With inadequate air circulation indoors, the soil remains wet longer. Also, some of their personnel are unfamiliar with succulents, and their watering often takes place on a large scale. These succulent plants end up taking in the same amount of water as non-drought-tolerant ones.

Identifying problems in a plant before taking it home will help you choose which ones to adopt. Starting with those that are not in their most excellent state is not a great way to start and can make your growing experience not only challenging but also discouraging.

You see, the way these plants look can be deceiving. For beginners, it is hard to detect the problem.

Overwatered succulents look lush and healthy at first. As the plants take in water, their storage spaces become filled, and they look greener, plumper, and more robust.

As they remain sitting on wet soil, absorption continues, and before you realize it, the plants are mushy.

Allowing them to go on absorbing water will lead you to fail.

Too much water can damage their water storage to a severe level. When that takes place, the injury is within and is hard to repair.

Sometimes, Less Is More!

Less frequent watering.
More chances of survival.
More chances for success.

It is also better to give less than to give more than what it can hold.

It is not because these plants do not like water. It is because they smartly control water. Different from the familiar plants we know.

For typical leafy plants, watering regularly and keeping the soil moist makes them happy. But succulent plants do not like it that way.

Their capacity to store is great when it comes to water. The roots will go on absorbing as long as they have access to it. That's their role, and they are great at it.

Succulents are brilliant at conserving water, but they are not very good at getting rid of excess. As more water gets stored, and a minimal amount escapes, a succulent's storage cells become so full, they get damaged.

Therefore, be in control of their access to water, if possible. Learn how to assess your plants and understand their needs.

Because there is a limit on how much water succulents can hold, check the plant and examine all the aspects that can cause overwatering.

What To Do When You Get Succulent Plants

So you picked up some succulents. Now what?

When can I water?
Can I plant cuttings right away?
Can I water them after planting?
Can I expose them to full sun?
Do I need to change the soil?

These are just a few questions some people ask when they get succulents for the first time.

Unfortunately, there's no general answer that applies to everyone.

Your initial step depends on how you obtained the plants and their overall condition.

First, what do you have? Succulent cuttings or with roots?

If they are cuttings, where did you get them? Are they fresh cuttings from your good neighbor, or you got them by mail?

If they are rooted, are they bare roots or with soil? Is it from a small pot or root bound?

Did you hand-pick it from an outdoor nursery exposed to full sun, or you got it inside your favorite DIY store?

How does the plant look?
Are the leaves plump or wrinkly?
Is the soil wet or dry?
Did you notice any pest, ants, or anything unusual?

It seems like a number of queries, but trust me, it's not that complicated.

Succulents can enter our lives in different ways, as fresh cuttings locally or through plant mail, bare-root through online purchases, in pots with soil, plucked leaves, and even seeds. Whichever way you are getting them from, they always bring us joy. Take a moment to enjoy whatever you do with them, either planting, creating projects, or propagating.

Cuttings

Growing succulents from cuttings is the cheapest way to start this hobby. You may have a very generous neighbor, a friend, or a co-worker who can spare you some from her garden. You can also order them online and get several varieties in one order at a price way cheaper than those with roots.

As a beginner, you might feel uncomfortable starting this way. But seriously, it is effortless. Try it, and you will be happy you did.

You are dealing with unique plants. The kind that will not wilt for weeks, or a month even, without soil or water. That which will continue living and survive neglect. They will grow roots on top of a dry paper towel or newspaper unattended.

You do not need to use soil all the time. You can use these cuttings for your soilless projects, like wreaths and frames or arrangements, using moss alone.

When you do this, the plant will focus on surviving and conserving its supply. Often, the plant will remain the same size, become dormant, and would hardly produce offsets.

Knowing which one can survive the longest can help you decide what to use for your projects. You can tell which ones will survive unfavorable situations by looking at their leaves.

The ones that will withstand the longest are those with chunky leaves and shiny, waxy leaf coatings, mostly from the Crassulaceae family, like *Crassula, Sedums,* and *Echeverias.* As the fresh wound heals, it seals the moisture inside the plant and remains plump.

Those with hairy covers, such as those with tomentose leaves and with thinner leaves, can also survive for more than two weeks, but they won't last as long. They will show signs of water deprivation after a while, like getting thinner and wrinkled.

Exposing them longer can completely deprive them of moisture and kill them.

When you use these cuttings, decide what you want to achieve. Would you like to use them in unique projects, or you want to propagate and grow more?

If you wish to expand your collection, then you need to plant the cuttings in the soil. Do not use just any soil, but fast-draining soil. We will discuss the proper soil mixture later in the following chapters.

HOW TO PLANT SUCCULENT CUTTINGS

When planting cuttings, let these tips guide you to success:

Allow the raw ends to callus before planting

Plant in containers with drainage

If you are dealing with fresh cuttings, the safest way is to allow the cut ends to callus for three to five days before planting in the soil. This initial step is critical, especially if the cuttings are small and plump.

Additional moisture taken up by the plant, either from its open wound or from the environment, will cause it to become mushy.

For bigger, fresh cuttings, you can plant right away, but make sure the soil is just moist or almost dry and not wet.

For those received via mail, the number of days they've spent inside the box during transit should be enough to callus. You've waited long enough for their arrival. You deserve to enjoy them.

So plant.

If you plan to plant them in individual containers, plant them in pots just slightly bigger than the plant. By doing so, it will help you avoid giving too much water in the future. Planting them together in one pot is another way to prevent giving too much, but carefully select those with the same watering requirements.

Again, judge the size and texture of their leaves. Terracotta pots and wooden planters are breathable and much preferred. You can also use planters other than regular pots as long as they have drainage holes.

Be more creative.

Do not water right away

I always advise people to wait for two weeks before watering. Around this time, some fast-growing plants will have small roots. But, when watering, it is always wise to look at the leaves of the plant and decide if they need water. If they still look bloated, wait for another week.

Do not expose to direct sunlight

Never expose your cuttings to direct sunlight. The bright shade is sufficient. They are not stable yet and couldn't protect themselves. Let them stabilize and become fully rooted before introducing them to full sun. And even though the plants are fully matured, it is still necessary to allow the plant to adjust slowly before full sun exposure to avoid sunburn.

What To Expect

A few days after planting succulent cuttings in the soil, you'll notice some changes. Some colorful cuttings may slowly revert to green. That should not be a problem because once they are stable, they can be slowly exposed to full sun and hopefully become colorful again if your location will permit. Expect some cuttings to perk up the next day after planting in the soil, especially if your soil is a bit moist.

Potted Plants

Nurseries usually sell succulents planted in plastic pots. If you are a beginner, try potted succulents first because they will have roots and be more stable.

Before you purchase, establish where you intend to use these plants. If you prefer the plants indoors, find those that will flourish in low-light conditions. If you have a sunny spot in your backyard, maybe choosing the kind that would change color when in full sun would be fun.

Most succulents are sun-loving plants. Though they will involve minimal care, most of them will need a lot of sunlight. So, find out the light requirements of your plant. Will the plant thrive in low-light conditions, or will it need full sun? The most colorful species will need full sun, which means unfiltered light for six to eight hours every day to maintain their color.

For indoors, locate a spot in your house where it can get bright light during the day. Otherwise, provide grow lights.

These plants come in various-sized containers, from small two-inch plastic pots to gallon sizes.

So You Bought Them. What Next?

If you prefer them indoors, in pots, you can look for a beautiful container to hold and display it without disturbing the roots. The plastic pot it came with already has holes, so if you find containers without drainage, it is okay to use those. Just remember to ensure that water won't pool at the bottom of the pot when you water.

Simple. Right?

You can also transfer the plant to a bigger pot, but choose a planter that is one size larger than your plant. A container that is too big can lead you to overwater, if you are not using the right soil mixture.

Loosen up the root ball and add soil designed for drought-smart plants. You do not need to take out all the dirt. We will have a chapter later dedicated to the soil mixture.

If you intend to use it for outdoor landscapes, resist the temptation to expose the plant to harsh direct sunlight right away without giving time to acclimatize because they can get sunburned.

You can likewise play around and create arrangements using rooted succulents. You can mix them with other succulent plants.

But How Do You Know Which Plants To Put Together?

When growing these plants together in one vessel, do not regard solely their aesthetic appeal. You must take into consideration the plant's watering needs. Avoid mixing plants needing frequent watering with those that don't. Otherwise, later on, some would look lush and healthy, and others would show signs of miserable health.

The simplest way to identify which ones to put together is by finding out what family the plant belongs to. Those from the Crassulaceae family are efficient at conserving water and flourish well in highly challenging locations.

Another way to identify them is by their leaves. Those with fleshy leaves and glossy, waxy coatings can go more prolonged stretches of drought and can keep more water. Those with fine hairs and with non-waxy cuticles are not as efficient in holding water.

You also need to consider their light requirements. Combining plants with low-light requirements to those needing full sun can either cause sunburn or etiolation. Exposing them to full sun will make sun-loving species happy, but will damage the leaves of those needing low light. In the same way, placing them in shady locations can make those with low-light needs happy, and others would elongate.Their mature size matters, too. Those that grow big can overpower those that are low-growing, those that can grow taller can outgrow others faster.

Did You Know That Plants Can Recognize Their Relatives?
Yes, they can tell if the adjacent roots are a stranger's or their relative's. When they are in the same pot with that of their kin, they restrain themselves. They avoid becoming competitive, and they share resources.

Bare-Root Succulents

Plants sent through mail often come bare root. Most soil is taken out, and the plant is wrapped, placed in a box, and posted.

The minute you receive this, inspect the plant for any pests or breaks. If the roots are moist when packed, the lack of airflow and excess humidity can promote the growth of mildew. Some leaves can become weak and will be soft and mushy when exposed to moisture inside the box for days.

Assuming what you received is absolutely dry, the leaves should remain plump and healthy. If they are somewhat wrinkly, do not worry, it will recover soon after planting in the soil and watering.

There's a therapy some people do when they get bare-root plants. You might have come across this online, and although I do not do this, it's worth discussing to give you some clarity.

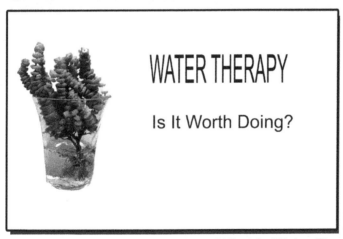

Some hacks work, and some can do further damage.

Performing water therapy is an immediate fix to a seriously dehydrated succulent, but can cause the life of the plant if not carried out right. For those who are battling to avoid overwatering, this can be a mind-boggling treatment that will leave you indeed further confused with succulents.

What Is Water Therapy?

This technique involves immersing the naked roots of succulent plants in water for a specific time. Usually within twenty-four hours or more. Plants that are wrinkly and badly dehydrated can bounce back from this therapy. Submerging the plant's roots in water is a quick process of restoring the water that the plant requires. But before you do water therapy, ask yourself why you want to do it and what do you wish to achieve. And is it worth it?

Positive Results

When you do water therapy, you will see fast results. You will notice the wrinkly succulents becoming plump and looking healthy. As the roots get submerged in water, they will absorb and fill up their storage spaces with water. It will surely result in a plump, healthy-looking plant. It is a quick and instant fix. Within twenty-four hours, a considerable improvement will be evident.

Although it might make you rejoice, you have to think twice. The outstanding result might be short-lived.

Possible Complication

The roots of the plant can get damaged during the process. As you soak it in water, it can soften. Just like what happens when you soak your feet in water for too long. Not to mention the higher risk of absorbing too much water. It can grow more roots as you soak in water, but this is not the quality of roots you need.

For long-term results, you need healthy roots. The kind that will not harden or become woody when all the moisture is depleted.

What To Watch Out For

Initially, the plant will look plump, but you might run into problems later on. When planted in the soil, it will remain fat for weeks. The water it has absorbed will sustain it. Once the stored water gets used up, it can look wrinkly. If, after watering several occasions, the condition does not improve, the roots might have been damaged.

Remember, succulents are not water plants. To safely care for these plants, you need to take into consideration that they came from arid regions. Nature does not provide them water in this manner.

What Then Is The Ideal Approach To Handle A Dehydrated Succulent?

When you get a bare-root succulent that looks dehydrated, plant it right away and water well. Allow the soil to dry thoroughly and evaluate the plant again. If it still remains wrinkly, water again. You will bring back the plant to good health in a slow but sure process.

CHAPTER FOUR

SOIL AND CONTAINERS

Have you been searching
for the best soil formula
for your succulents?

The Soil Of Champions

Using the right kind of soil and planters is essential for growing succulents. It is as important as applying the proper watering technique. Fast-draining soil and adequate drainage must go together, as both are vital. You can have the best soil mixture, but without the proper drainage, you'll see subpar results. The same is true when you have suitable drainage holes but compacted soil. The plants' roots will find it hard to access water when the soil is hard. Knowing the right materials and the reason for their use can help you achieve success.

Soil is a mixture of organic and inorganic components. It contains minerals, gases, liquids, and organisms that together support the life of a plant. Organic matter has already decomposed and is resistant to further decomposition. Organic material, however, is anything alive before that is now in or on the soil that can still decompose. They are natural materials, such as peat moss, compost, or composted manure or crop residues. Organic components provide nutrients to the plants. They also absorb and hold water and release it back to the plant. The inorganic materials of soil are rocks broken down into smaller particles of different sizes, sand, silt, and clay.

After visiting different nurseries and talking to several gardeners, I realized that none of them use the same mixtures. But, guess what, they all grow healthy succulents.

Plant roots are composed of living cells; they need to remain healthy to function well. They are responsible for water uptake and anchor the plants in place. To continue being healthy, roots need oxygen. Of course, plants take in carbon dioxide and give off oxygen. But the oxygen that we are talking about here is to supply the roots. The roots need to respire to remain healthy.

Roots do a lot of work absorbing water and nutrients and pressurizing the plant enough for the water and nutrients to reach the leaves. The process requires energy, and in turn, requires oxygen. When the roots are sick, it will affect the health of your plants.

There are bacteria present in the soil that help increase nutrient availability to plants by dissolving elements and making them available for plants to take in. Microorganisms are beneficial to the health of the plants, as they are the primary decomposers of organic materials.

What Kind Of Soil Should You Avoid?

Avoid Compacted Soil

In compacted soil, particles are pressed together, leaving small spaces in between. These conditions can suffocate roots. Compaction occurs mostly in heavier soil, like clay. Fine mineral particles with few organic materials comprise this type of soil. This type of dirt is sticky. When soil is compacted, roots cannot push through to find water and nutrients.

Tight soil can also restrict the movement of water into the soil. Water may settle on top but not reach the bottom. But breaking up the soil by adding sand will not fully solve the problem. Fine sand can make soil even more compact. You need larger particles when you condition your soil. When amending the soil, add large particles of inorganic materials. You can use coarse sand, perlite, pebbles, pumice, or Turface.

Avoid Waterlogged Soil

Soil is waterlogged when it is saturated with water most of the time. This occurs because the soil does not drain well or the container does not have enough drainage. With too much water in the soil, the air pockets get filled with water, suffocating the roots. Over time, the plant will be deprived of oxygen, develop root rot, and die.

Good bacteria in the soil that thrives in the presence of oxygen will die when there's no more oxygen. Then, harmful bacteria grow and attack the roots, causing them to rot.

Why Create Your Soil Mixture?

Mixing your soil for succulents is easy and is cheaper than buying ready-made cactus mix. You can also use what is available in your area if you are aware of what alternatives you can use. Adjust the mixture until you find the best fit for your plants' needs. You can control the texture based on what you want to achieve. If it does not drain fast enough, you can add more inorganic material until you are happy with the outcome.

By experimenting, you can create a mix that best suits your plants' needs.

What Kind Of Soil Mixture Should You Use?

You need to create a soil mix that will dry fast. It must drain well but also allow the root time to absorb water. Always think of where these plants came from and provide that kind of environment. In the desert, the soil is often dry. If it rains, it is usually brief, and the soil dries out fast because of evaporation. The ground is porous, so air and water can pass through it with less effort, and it dries in no time, too. You should aim for a soil mixture with a good crumbly structure to ensure proper drainage.

Here's our formula for the soil we use for our succulents. It is a 50 percent organic and 50 percent inorganic mix.

Here's our formula for the soil we use for our succulents. It is a 50 percent organic and 50 percent inorganic mix.

Chopstick and Succulents (KISS Formula)
Keep It Simple Soil Formula

Potting Soil   **Coarse Sand**   **Perlite**

I always try to make things simple, so I go with only three ingredients, which I can buy from home and garden centers:

Two parts potting soil.

One part perlite.

One part coarse sand.

This formula has worked well for me. It has provided me with a medium that my plants like in my location here in California. You don't need to use the same formula. You can always adjust your mix and create your version of what is available in your location. Remember to check that your mixture drains fast. Adjust depending on your location and plant variety.

How To Check If The Soil Drains Fast

Mix all the components in a container and pour water over the mixture. Observe the rate at which the water drains.

Within fifteen to twenty seconds, the water should all go down and not stay on top of the soil. If the water seeps through fast, then you have a fast-draining mixture.

You can also do a clump test by taking a handful of the mixture and squeezing it in your hand. It should not form a lump but rather crumble. If it sticks together, you need to adjust the mixture by adding more inorganic materials. To improve drainage, add perlite, pumice, or lava rocks.

Below are the materials you can use as a substitute when you create the fast-draining soil mixture for your succulent plants. Remember the fifty percent organic and fifty percent inorganic mixture, and you can adjust according to your location.

ORGANIC

Garden Soil

Compost

Vermicast

Coco Peat

Bark

Carbonized Rice Hull

Potting Soil

INORGANIC

Perlite

Coarse Sand

Pumice

Turface

Poultry Grit

Pebbles

Lava Rocks

Containing Your Joy

Gardening with succulents is possible even with limited space. Most succulents have shallow roots and are slow-growers, making them ideal plants for container gardens.

There are so many varieties to select, but it all depends on the project you have in mind. There are those ideal for indoors, like *Sansevierias* and *Haworthias*, which require low light. Some change colors depending on the treatment they receive.

They are impressive when mixed with other species but can also be elegant on their own. Even a single succulent in a very simple planter can look charming.

Working with succulents can take your imagination and creativity to the next level. You can be like a child again by creating fairy gardens.

You can create vertical projects, like living wall frames and ledges, and hang them. You can incorporate them into your holiday decor or centerpieces. As a bonus, you can share them and give them as gifts, either as cuttings or in an arrangement. With succulents, you can show off your personal touch as well as your creative style.

Know that there are countless ways to display succulents. They do not need to be in a container.

They can be on an old chair or a bench—pretty much anywhere that can hold some soil or moss on its own.

But not everyone is comfortable planting succulents anywhere. Some of these plants are quite pricey. When one is new to this hobby, successfully growing them is the utmost priority. So, let's begin with where many people are more comfortable growing plants—in containers.

Containers come in different materials, shapes, and textures. Each has its advantages and disadvantages. Beyond having aesthetic value, containers can affect the plants they hold. One major problem is when water cannot drain from a container. When a planter lacks drainage holes, water can collect at the bottom of the pot. When water is stagnant, it can lead to waterlogged soil. This condition is not healthy for your succulent plants.

Their weight can be an issue, too. When the planters are too heavy, moving them around can be a problem. If you live where you need to move plants inside during winter, heavy planters may not be practical.

The different types of containers have advantages and disadvantages. Use this guide to decide which one is good for you and your plants.

Clay Pots

Unglazed clay pots are best for your succulents. Clay pots provide a healthy environment for plants because of their porosity. This allows air and moisture to penetrate at the side of the container, allowing the soil to breathe. What's more, clay wicks moisture away from the soil. Since succulents prefer their roots dry rather than wet, this is an ideal setup. If you tend to overwater, these pots may be beneficial for you.

The walls of terracotta pots are thick and add extra protection to plant roots. They can insulate and protect them from rapid changes in environmental temperatures. Terracotta pots are also sturdy enough that they won't tip over when the plant is not balanced.

They are suitable for indoors but also great for outdoors. Terracotta, with its brownish-orange color, has a rustic appeal. It blends well in a garden. These pots are available in different sizes. The bigger ones can be costly, but the smaller ones are very affordable. The downside of the bigger containers is that they are heavy. Adding more soil, plants, and water can make them difficult to move.

Furthermore, terracotta pots may look strong and sturdy, but they are fragile. These planters chip or break, but they also can also crack as the clay expands or contracts with temperature changes. Over time, you might notice some whitish deposits on the outer walls of these pots. These are the mineral salts wicked from the soil and that passed through the side of the pot.

Wood And Basket Planters

Their beauty will never run out of style. Wood not only brings natural rustic charm, but it also insulates the plant from heat. It is also porous and allows excess moisture to escape from the soil. Drilling a hole for drainage is easy, too. Their sensitivity to environmental factors like the sun, water, and frost is a disadvantage, however. Exposure to these elements can shorten their lifespan.

To ensure longevity, treat wood planters with nontoxic stains or water-proofing agents before use. Using a plastic lining for baskets can also help. If possible, use durable materials like cedar and oak, as they have a natural resistance to rot. Redwood or teak are also good choices. Otherwise, seal it.

When placed on the ground, protect them from direct contact with the soil to prevent rot.

Resin Planters

Designed to withstand wear and tear, these planters won't chip or break. This material is not short on durability. Made of nonporous material, it does not absorb stains and is not affected by the elements. While native planters discolor with prolonged exposure to the sun, resins will not. It will last for years without maintenance.

They can look expensive and natural, but their prices can vary, often depending on size. Being lightweight, they are easy to transport, especially compared to large clay planters.

Metal Containers

Metal is not the ideal material to hold your succulent plants. Although they won't crack or break, cheap metals can rust, and thin ones can dent. A metal container won't provide insulation for the roots when the temperature changes. Under the hot sun, metal can heat up, which can cause damage to parts of the plant in contact with the metal.

They are also non porous. Drilling a hole is necessary but not difficult.

Concrete Planters

Concrete is durable and will last a long time, and because it is cumbersome, it is less likely to topple during strong winds. The thickness and lighter color of these planters help protect plants from temperature fluctuations. Concrete is also porous, allowing air and water to escape from the sides.

You can also be more creative and design your pots with concrete. There are a lot of DIY videos online about how to create these types of projects, if they interest you.

Can You Use Containers Without Drainage Holes?

We learn that the drainage hole is vital to ensure the health of the plants. Yet, there are circumstances where drilling a hole is just not achievable.

In using glass containers for a terrarium, for example, drilling a hole can lead to the glass breaking. Sometimes the container is so fragile that you don't wish to risk breaking it by drilling a hole.

Yes, you can use containers without drainage holes for your projects. And yes, it's not going to hurt your plants as long as you avoid the detrimental effects of not allowing the water to drain.

First, understand why it can cause damage to the plants and identify measures to resolve the problem.

Here's what could take place when succulents are grown in vessels without drainage:

*The plants can receive too much water.
*Their roots will sit on wet soil for too long.
*Anaerobic bacteria can grow and attack the roots of the plants, causing the plant to rot.

Solving The Problem

Overwatered succulents can die. It can happen when the plant gets more water than it can hold.

To avoid giving too much water, be in control of the amount of water they receive. Keep in mind that the plant will most likely absorb the whole amount you poured.

So, look at the size of your plant and its current hydration status and estimate the amount you give that is just enough not to hurt it.

You should not soak it when you water, and make sure to protect it from the rain.

Waterlogged Soil

If you let succulents sit in the wet ground too long, not only will they absorb too much water, but soil saturated in water also deprives the roots of their much-needed oxygen. Using very shallow containers with wide openings can help solve this problem.

With shallow containers, the soil can dry out fast. In deep containers, water can pool at the bottom. The soil on top may look and feel dry. It can mislead you to decide it is time to water, but underneath, it is still wet, and the roots still have access to water.

Another way to avoid this problem is to give only enough water that will dry out fast. Enough that it will dry in a day or two.

Work with your environment, if your plant is outdoors, with good air circulation, you can give a bit more water than those you placed indoors. Also, adjust your watering based on your climate and withhold water during winter.

Growth Of Harmful Bacteria

When too much water gathers too long in the soil, you'll notice a strong rotten smell. Remember that healthy soil consists of air pockets that allow plant roots to breathe. There are also healthy bacteria living in it.

Soil saturated in water displaces air pockets as well as killing the good bacteria that thrive in the presence of oxygen. Such an environment becomes a happy place for harmful bacteria to grow.

To avoid the problem, add a layer of activated charcoal under the soil or beneath the layer of pebbles. It will help absorb extra water and remove odors. It will also act as a filter that will pull out toxins and bacteria.

Other Ways To Display Succulents

CHAPTER
FIVE

Sunlight And Acclimatization

Recognizing Signs Of Overwatering

Keep in mind that succulent plants, even though labeled as full sun, should not be exposed to full sun right away after you acquire it. Especially when the heat of the sun is harsh, and you got them from a sheltered location, such as from an indoor nursery.

Sunlight and Acclimatization

Succulent plants require a particular level of sunlight exposure in order to flourish. Although most succulents are sun-loving, not all will do well in full sun.

When buying succulent plants, usually, there is a tag attached to it with directions concerning their needed sunlight exposures.

There are four main categories used to describe the amount of sunlight exposure the plant requires:

Full sun
Partial sun
Full shade
Partial shade

Now, before we differentiate these varying sunlight exposures, it is a must to keep in mind that succulent plants, even though labeled as full sun, should not be exposed to full sun right away after you acquire it. Especially when the heat of the sun is harsh, and you got them from a sheltered location, such as from an indoor nursery.

The abrupt change of location and strength of the sunlight can overwhelm the plants. They can get sunburn.

The only time you display your plant to full sunlight is when you are certain that the plant is perfectly adjusted to full sun exposure. For example, if you handpicked the plant from an outdoor nursery already exposed and adapted to the heat of the sun, it won't cause any damage.

Succulents getting sunburned is not merely ugly; it can kill your plants.

For us humans, we can put on some sunscreen to protect us immediately when we go out in the sun. But for some succulent plants, they require time to modify and develop their protective coating. When the degree of sunlight hurts your skin, it can possibly injure them, too.

You can identify when they get sunburned because there's an uneven discoloration on the leaves of the plant you just transferred to a new sunny site. You will likewise see pale, whitish-gray, or dark brown to black stain. The deeper the color, the more serious the burn.

Now, let's differentiate the degrees of sunlight exposure your plant requires.

Full Sun

Full sun
Your plant needs at least six full hours of direct or unfiltered light all day. The sun is direct, and there's no interference.

Part Sun

Partial sun
The plant needs three to six hours of sun exposure per day, preferably the cooler hours of the morning or early afternoon. They love the morning sun and can deal with some afternoon exposure. The plant is better tolerant of heat.

Full Shade

Full shade
Provide less than four hours of sunlight. Bright light but little or no direct sunlight.

Partial shade
The plant needs three to six hours of morning sunlight exposure per day but should be covered from the afternoon sun. This can be achieved by placing it near a tree that can cast afternoon shade and block the direct afternoon sun. Consider protection starting around 2 pm to 5 pm. The plant is less tolerant of heat.

How To Avoid Sunburn

Never expose the succulent for the first time to direct noontime sun, especially during the summer, where the heat is too harsh.

Even mature plants that are fully-rooted and stable, when moved from shade to direct sunlight when it is too hot, can get sunburned. I learned the hard way when I moved my two-feet-tall Crassula ovata to the full sun location when I did my landscaping last summer.

Anytime the heat of the sun hurts your skin, it can hurt them, too. When the heat is milder, it's safe to take them out anytime so that when summer comes, they are then adjusted.

Allowing them to adapt to the heat of the sun should not require too much effort on your part. You do not need to keep on moving them every day to increase their sun exposure. It simply requires you to find that spot that can provide sunlight in varying degrees. It does not mean moving them in and out of the sun either.

To simplify, I'm not going to use the four cardinal directions—north, east, south, and west—as we live in different locations.

The simplest way to do this is to locate a spot where the plant can receive morning sun consistently for two weeks.

Consistency is the key here. All you need is to allow the plant to get used to its new location. Aside from the fact that moving them in and out of the sun in a few-hour increments a day is a lot of work, you would be changing their location again when they just barely adjusted.

Your next step is to find a spot where you can shift the plant to receive morning and late afternoon sun but sheltered from the harsh early afternoon sun. It can be a protection from the shade of a tree or another taller plant. You can also cover them by using shade cloth. Leave the plant in the same location for two weeks.

What To Do When Succulents Get Sunburned

If the sunburn occurred that same day, transfer the plant to a spot with less light exposure. Allow it to settle for a few days and gently introduce it to the sun starting with morning light.

If you noticed the damage a few days later, and it is just mild, it is best to keep the plant in the same place. Whatever damage it incurred cannot be reverted. The marks will remain, but the plant will grow new leaves that are fully adjusted to the heat. Closely monitor your plant. If the damage remains the same and appears not to be progressing, there's no call for action.

Those that sustained blackish discolorations should be moved and set in an area away from direct sunlight. Allow them to rest.

Mild
Sunburn

Severe
Sunburn

Then, check the plant for sunburn. Those with pruinose leaves (pale powdery coating) should be further obvious. Those colorful species should show off more color, if your climate permits. Then you can move them to the full sun, where they can receive unobstructed sunlight the whole day.

Beware of reflective surfaces like walls or glass windows that can strengthen the heat of the sun. The reflected heat can damage their tender leaves, too.

When should you not expose your succulents to full sun?

When the plant is overwatered and weak.
Plants that have taken in too much water can have bloated leaves. As the leaves enlarge, their outer skin cover becomes thinner, causing their leaves to be more sensitive, and they can get sunburned.

When the plant is adapted to the shade.
Abrupt exposure to stronger light than what the plant is used to can damage their delicate leaves. Allow them to get used to the heat of the sun gradually.

When plants only require low light.
Those soft-leaved Haworthias do nicely in partial shade. Their leaves are vulnerable and can get damaged when in full sun exposure.

When cuttings are newly planted.
They are not sufficiently rooted and stable. The leaves can wilt. Their cut end is like a wound that is still raw and open.

When succulent leaf propagation hasn't sprouted babies.
Bright morning light is sufficient for their sunlight needs. Let the plant concentrate on growing new life without being exposed to much stress.

Overwatered and Sunburned Echeveria agavoides 'Lipstick'

Sunburned Echeveria gibbiflora

Seven Ways To Check For An Overwatered Succulents

1. Feel The Soil

The soil should be dry or damp but not soaking wet. These plants will continue absorbing water as long as they have access to it. If a plant is indoors, the soil may remain wet for days.

A very plump-looking succulent that continues to sit on wet soil can absorb more than it needs. The plant may seem healthy at first, but over time, you will see some unpleasant changes if not removed from that wet environment. If you are buying a new plant that looks bloated, and since you do not know how long it has been wet, it is best to avoid taking it home unless you know how to save it.

LEAVES DROPPING

2. Inspect For Dropping Leaves

Dropping leaves is not a good sign. It may mean that they've received more water than they need. You'll know it because the leaves will swell up and become so heavy they separate from the stem and fall off. Inspecting the plants to make sure that there are no dropping leaves at the base of the plant is helpful.

You might wonder, who would sell plants in this state?

But it is not uncommon to see underlit, almost-drowned succulents that look miserable in the corner of some indoor nurseries. Those who have been around succulent plants for a while can spot this problem right away. For beginners who don't know how to differentiate between a healthy-looking succulent and a plump succulent that is close to drowning, this can be hard.

Be aware that there are succulents with leaves that can drop off from their stem. Examples are *Graptoverias* and some *Sedums*. If you are not sure why leaves are falling, keep on searching for more signs.

Dropped leaves with intact tips are the best specimens for propagation, by the way. When they are soft and mushy, however, the whole leaf is damaged and can no longer produce a new life.

Echeveria runyonii 'Topsy Turvy'

Echeveria 'Lola'

3. Observe The Rosette

Succulents come in a variety of shapes and colors. I'm sure you love those rosette-forming *Echeverias*, too. They usually grow close to the ground to capture the moisture.

The way their leaves behave can tell you if they need more water or have had too much. The *Echeveria runyonii* 'Topsy Turvy,' for example, has a rosette that is tight and wavy. When overwatered, it opens up like a flower in full bloom. The waves are almost gone as it stretches out to accommodate more water.

NORMAL / OVERWATERED

Fenestraria rhopalophylla 'Baby Toes'

Senecio rowleyanus 'String of Pearls'

4. Note For Presence Of Cracks

This unique-shaped succulent looks like the toes of an infant, hence the name 'Baby Toes.' They are native to South Africa, where they grow unattended in the wild. The weather is dry most of the time, with very little rainfall.

They have coped well in a hot, arid environment by burying part of their bodies underground. Baby Toes have shallow roots and grow best in narrow containers with good drainage. It is safer to withhold watering for a time, as they can tolerate a bit of neglect better than being watered too soon.

The epidermal window on top of their leaves can tell you their hydration status. It becomes thin and shiny as it stretches out to hold more water. This looks like a blister that is about to pop. If it can no longer hold, it will crack.

When this happens, rescue the plant from its location as soon as possible. The damaged area may not be salvageable, but other parts can. It is vital to keep it dry now and remove it from any source of water.

Keep it safe by keeping it dry, and be very careful the next time you water.

Echeveria gibbiflora 'Ruffles'

Echeveria 'Atlantis'

5. Colorful Variety Turning Green

When succulents are overwatered, they are no longer stressed and they also change color. The colorful varieties revert to green.

One unique characteristic of succulents is their ability to change colors when stressed. The environment influences a succulent's change of colors. Sun, water, humidity, and temperature contribute to this change. Changing color is their way of protecting themselves from the harmful rays of the sun, cold temperatures, or not having enough water.

Senecio haworthii
'Cocoon Plant'

These wooly covers are not very elastic
and can tear when the leaves expand.

6. Their Wooly Covers May Tear

Succulents' wooly covers help trap moisture and keep them cooler. The light-colored cotton-like cover reflects the sunlight and protects them from heat. As their leaves expand, so do their outer coverings. When too tight, this covering tears off like a cloth.

7. Presence Of Soft, Mushy Leaves

Overwatering is not only the most common cause of failure in raising succulents. It is also, by a considerable margin, the most deadly. It is a grave mistake from which a plant might not recover.

The presence of soft, translucent leaves indicates over-watering. Too much water can cause the storage cell walls to leak, and fluid can seep out. This can cause discoloration and soft, squishy leaves. As the leaves soften, they will easily detach from the stem. When squeezed, fluids will escape from their thinned outer skin cover.

Dry and crisp leaves at the base of the plant are normal, but if you see soft, mushy leaves that are turning yellow, brown, or black, it is not good.

CHAPTER SIX

**How To Water Succulents
Special Tricks That Work**

Not knowing how to water succulents correctly is a pretty common problem, especially for those just starting this succulent hobby. Knowing when it is time to water and how much to give is essential to keeping these plants alive. The more they are watered like common house plants, the more they do not like it. It is not because they do not like water. It is because they handle water differently.

Did you know that you can control the growth of your succulent plants based on how you water them? The more water you give, the faster they grow. When watered less, the slower they grow; they become dormant and conserve their supply to survive.

So, when you plant, determine what you want to achieve. If you want a plant to remain small, like a succulent bonsai, plant it in a small, shallow pot with less soil to hold water and do not provide nutrients. Longer gaps in between watering can also help you achieve that purpose.

If you plan to propagate more to increase your collection, you need to plant in bigger pots or in the ground, fertilizing and watering often to encourage new growth. You can do this without killing your plants by making sure they still have room to store water. The key is to only give your plants enough water to fill them.

Most succulent plants are native to desert-like locations. They are good at conserving their water supply to survive drought. In the desert, it seldom rains—maybe only once or twice a year. But when it rains, it pours, and water evaporates fast, too. So, to mimic such an environment, allow the soil to completely dry before watering again. And when you water, water thoroughly. You want to make sure that the water penetrates the soil and reaches the roots.

That's why misting is not recommended for that reason. When you mist, you wet only the top soil, and water barely reaches the roots. Most of the water will also evaporate, with little to no benefit to the plant. What you need is for the plants to take in all the water it can store for their future use.

Although watering a plant thoroughly is highly recommended to encourage healthy plants, this does not always apply to all your succulents. When succulents are placed indoors, in larger containers, the soil may remain wet for days because of a lack of ventilation. When succulents sit in wet soil, they absorb more water than what they can tolerate, or their roots soften and rot. In that case, watering just enough so that the soil will dry out in a day or two is more appropriate than completely soaking the soil.

That is why it is important to assess your plants and determine how to water them so they will receive just the right amount of water to keep them plump while keeping their roots dry.

In some nurseries, they water as often as every three days during summer because they want the plant to get bigger faster for a better return on investment. They can do so without too much worry, especially if the weather helps dry the soil out fast. Remember, the more you water, the faster succulents grow, and when watered less, they concentrate on conserving it to survive.

In other locations where it is more humid, with occasional rain showers, watering as often as this can cause the plants to rot and their leaves to crack. It is all because of their storage as well as the length of time that the soil is wet.

I know, I've mentioned this several times, and I will remind you again. Succulents store water in their leaves, roots, or stems. It is important to identify where your succulents store water and how much space is available, because their storage spaces have limitations.

The size of the plant also impacts how much water is enough to fill up its storage. On top of that, there are other factors that can affect the amount of water absorbed, such as the amount of water your soil mixture can hold, the length of time the roots have access to water, or the amount of water that evaporates after watering.

A plant that has countless succulent leaves and a large trunk can tolerate a lot of water, including heavy rains, without issue. But a small succulent plant with five to ten leaves may receive too much even if watered only once per week. To put it simply, bigger plants, bigger storage spaces, more water is tolerated. Smaller plants, limited storage spaces, and can only tolerate minimal amounts.

The size of their storage can also affect how often you should water. When a plant is thick and fleshy, it can store a lot of water and can go longer periods without adding more to it. But those with thinner leaves have limited space and might need a small amount of water each time but need to be refilled more frequently.

Succulents' ability to conserve water can also affect the frequency of watering. Those with waxy coatings, such as *Crassula ovata*, can lose less moisture than hairy ones like *Cotyledon tomentosa* 'Bear's Paw.'

What's interesting is that when the roots detect drought, succulents try to conserve and change. You'll see their colors change and their metabolic activity slow down. The same thing when there is an abundance of water. The plant becomes vegetative, and they grow bigger and greener.

But when their storage space is full, the roots do not stop absorbing, and the pores won't open more to get rid of excess. Their storage space simply expands to accommodate more water.

Luckily, even though you cannot see what is going on inside the cells, the plant can tell you if it's had too much water. There are signs that you can watch out for: bloated leaves, rosettes opening and expanding, and a greener and more vegetative appearance. The succulent may also feel hard when touched, have cracked or split leaves, or worse, have mushy and translucent leaves. In this last case, the damage is within the cells. Cells have walls, and when burst open, they can leak to the surrounding tissues, leading to soft, translucent, mushy leaves.

In short, these plants are good at conserving water, but they cannot say no to water as long as it is present. When the soil is dry, the roots send a signal to the plant to conserve and protect its water supply. But when the storage cells are full of water, the roots cannot detect it and will continue absorbing.

Water is such a temptation that they cannot resist. As a caretaker of this plant, it is your responsibility to control their access to water.

Knowing the right time to water and how much water to give is important to successfully grow these plants. Also, not all succulents have the same watering requirements. How will you know when it is time, and how much should you give?

Overwatering can be so serious that a plant might not be able to recover from it. With succulents, it is better to give less than more. You can always give them water again after a few days if they still need more. But if you have a succulent that's absorbed too much, how can you take it back?

When Should You Not Water?

You should not water if your plant looks bloated; if the rosettes are wide open and expanding; if the succulent is discolored with yellowing or translucent leaves; if the epidermal window is getting thinner and bulging; or if you notice the leaves dropping. And of course, don't water your outdoor succulents if rain is forecasted.

Bloated Leaves

Wide Open Rosette

Expanding Leaves

Translucent Leaves

Bulging or Cracked Leaves

Leaves Falling-off

How Will You Know When It Is Time To Water?

Start with an inspection. Look at the leaves of your plants. If they show signs of dehydration, like wrinkled leaves, it is time to water.

But you do not need to wait for the leaves to get wrinkly before watering. A healthy-looking succulent plant can be watered safely after seven to ten days as long as they have room for more water and by making sure that the amount of water you give will dry out in a day or two.

Of course, you have to ensure that the soil is completely dry. If you are using the proper soil mixture for your succulent plants, it should be completely dry in three days.

Remember, the plant's water storage is not completely depleted; you just want to refill them to keep them looking plump and healthy. Keep in mind that there are succulent plants, like Lithops, that are more sensitive to water and have different watering needs.

Apply the water balloon technique if you are still not sure after your visual inspection. Try to feel the lower-most leaf, and do this only as a last recourse, as you do not want to damage the waxy coatings that is there to protect them.

A Special Trick That Works: Feel A Leaf Like A Water Balloon

If you are still not certain whether your succulent needs water, feel it and imagine a water balloon. You can tell if a balloon is full of air or water because it feels hard. When there is still space to add more, you can indent it with your fingers when you slightly press it down.

But a very full balloon feels hard, and adding more to it might cause it to pop.

The same principle applies for succulents. If one is already full of water, adding more to it can cause the leaves to crack or the cell walls to tear. Try to feel a leaf and treat it as a balloon filled with water. Slightly press it down. If it feels hard, then (obviously) there's no more room for water, and adding more could be damaging. But if the leaf feels soft, or if you can slightly indent it when you press it down, you have more room to fill.

If you can tell how a full balloon feels, you can do the same with the leaves of your succulents—with exception to those spiky cacti, of course.

How Often Should You Water?

The frequency of watering depends on the individual plant. Some can hold water longer and might not need to be watered as often. The most common frequency is once a week during the summer and once a month during winter.

Again, it all depends on your plants and your location.

Here in California, where it is always sunny and the humidity is low, we can water twice a week during the summer, and the plants will be healthy. This is because most of our plants are outdoors, where water evaporates fast.

During winter, we water once a month sparingly and sometimes even skip watering. You'll be surprised, but these plants can survive for months without being watered. They may not look plump, but they will keep on living. It is what they are good at— surviving when water is scarce.

Giving your plants water depending on their needs is the safest and most effective way to keep your succulents thriving. Always consider your plants' individual needs. Figuring out when and how much to give is what you need to master. It might not be easy at first, but once you follow these steps, you will soon find it easy.

Do not water your plants without checking them first. The dryness of the soil is not the best indicator that they need to be watered. Although it is important for the soil to dry out completely in between watering, if the soil remains wet for a longer period, you might need to amend your soil mixture. Consider adding more inorganic materials like perlite, pumice, or coarse sand to keep your soil from being too wet after watering.

In the same way, tracking the time since you last watered your succulents is not a foolproof plan. Your plants' watering needs will vary depending on your location and the weather. Always look at the plants and decide if they need to be watered.

When Is The Best Time To Water?

Water in the morning when it is still cooler to help keep water evaporation to a minimum. This will allow the roots to absorb more water without competing as much with the environment.

For succulents outdoors, with the heat during the day and good air circulation, the soil can dry out on the same day, and the plant will not be sitting on wet soil in the evening. This is also important if you want to maintain the vibrant colors of your plants. By giving your succulents just enough water, you'll have soil that will dry out that same day, keeping the soil completely dry in between waterings.

Avoid watering during midday during the intense heat of the sun. Not only are you wasting water, as most of it will be lost through evaporation, water beads that settle on the leaves may act as a magnifier and can cause sunburn, especially when the heat of the sun is so intense.

In some locations, it can get above one hundred degrees Fahrenheit during summer. Watering succulents during the intense heat of the sun can cause damage and is not good for them. So, wait until it cools down before you water.

When you anticipate three-digit temperature the next day, water your plants thoroughly the day before and prepare to shelter them by providing shade.

How Much Water To Give

Deciding how much water to give depends on several factors: plant genus, size, hydration status, soil mixture, container, and climate. Let's go through these one by one.

Plant Genus

Although all succulents store water, they vary in how efficient they are at holding this and in how they accomplish it. Some varieties with thick, waxy leaves can hold water longer than others with non-waxy leaves. Those with plump, fleshy leaves can hold more water than those with thin leaves and therefore can be given more. Those with thinner leaves will benefit from smaller amounts of water but more frequent watering.

Be aware that some varieties, such as the *Senecio peregrinus* 'String of Dolphins' and *Senecio rowleyanus* 'String of Pearls,' do well in soil that is a bit moist rather than completely dry. But again, always look at the overall condition of the plant.

When exposed to prolonged sunlight without adequate watering, succulents with thinner leaves may completely use up their supply, drying and turning crispy. Those with more storage may be more resilient, change colors, and become dormant to reduce their metabolic activity.

Plant Size

Always take into account the size of your plants and where they store water. The bigger the plant, the more space to store water. When a plant is small, they also have small storage spaces.

Your newly bought succulent, for example, might be a small-rooted cutting and will therefore need only a small amount of water. However, a mature, well-established plant growing on the ground or in a large container will have numerous leaves and a larger trunk, and can, therefore, tolerate even heavy rains.

Corpuscularia lehmannii 'Ice Plant'

Plant Hydration Status

An obviously dehydrated plant will have wrinkled leaves and will benefit from a good soak.

You do not need to wait for the plant to show these signs before giving them water. If the plant looks healthy and you want to maintain it, give it water, but only an amount that will dry out in a day. Remember, they still have stored water inside, and you just want to add enough to fill those spaces. Succulent plants with bloated leaves should not be given water at all.

Soil Mixture

The soil mixture you use can affect the amount of water absorbed. When you use soil with more organic materials, more water is retained. When you use more inorganic materials with larger particles, more water drains through.

Plant roots take up water and food from the soil. They also need air to breathe. When your soil is constantly wet, as is the case with waterlogged soil, there won't be many air pockets, so the roots will be deprived of oxygen.

Ideally, your soil should be dry two to three days after watering. If your soil is not yet dry after days of not being watered, you might need to find a way to amend it. This kind of soil is not the ideal mixture for your plants. You need soil that will drain faster and not hold too much moisture. When roots have access to moisture, they will continue to absorb.

If you are using a gritty mix that allows water to drain fast and retains a small portion for the plant to absorb, thoroughly wet it.

But if your soil mixture is what we recommend—a 50 percent organic and 50 percent inorganic mix—give only enough water to fill your plants' storage and adjust depending on where you place the plants.

CHAPTER SEVEN

SAVING OVERWATERED SUCCULENTS

WATERING INDOOR SUCCULENTS

WHAT YOUR PLANT IS TRYING TO TELL YOU

How To Save An Overwatered Succulent

What if you overwater your succulent plant or bought one that is dying from overwatering? Can you still save it?

The good news is, you can save these plant if you recognize the signs early and act right away. Even though the plant looks bad, there are still parts you can salvage. Do not give up and throw your plant away. Give it a chance and you'll be surprised by what you might see grow.

Remember, whatever water that has been absorbed cannot be taken back. Whatever damage that occurred cannot be reverted. But you can still save portions that are not yet damaged. This may be a few leaves or a portion of the trunk or roots. Succulents are survivors, and they can propagate from a single leaf, a broken branch, or their roots.

The first thing you need to do is to stop the roots from absorbing more water.

For an overwatered plant that does not show obvious signs of damage, place it in a well-ventilated area or in front of a fan to dry the soil quickly. Do not place overwatered succulents with wet soil indoors because it takes even longer for soil to dry inside.

If the soil is already dry, there's no need to uproot your succulent. Simply remove the damaged parts and place your succulent in partial shade. Do not expose your overwatered succulent to direct sunlight, especially during the summer when the sun is harsh. An overwatered succulent is already struggling, and exposing it to direct sunlight can add more damage.

If part of the plant is damaged, and the soil remains wet, here's what you can do:

Remove As Much Soil As Possible
Remove the plant from the source of water. Take the plant out of the pot and remove as much soil as possible, because the roots will continue

absorbing water. Change the soil medium to a fast-draining mix. It is easy to remove the soil when it is wet. Inspect the roots for the presence of root rot. If the roots are a soft brown and easily fall apart, remove them. Healthy roots are white or tan colored.

Air Dry
After removing the wet soil, place the succulent on top of a dry paper towel away from direct sunlight for a day or two. The plant will be fine without any soil. The water it has absorbed will keep it alive.

Plant On Dry Soil
Prepare your pot with a dry soil mixture and plant. You may also transplant your succulent after removing it from wet soil as long as the soil is dry.

Place In Part Shade
Provide three to six hours of sun, but protect the plant from the intense midday sun. Allow the plant to rest and recover.

Be Mindful The Next Time You Water
Make sure that the plant is ready to be watered the next time you give it a drink. Give only an amount that will dry out fast.

Your succulent may look dead, but you might get a surprise after letting it rest in a corner. I suggest forgetting about it to avoid being tempted to water again. Remember, it almost drowned because it had too much.

Growing Indoor Succulents

Growing indoor succulents can be more challenging compared to growing them outdoors. Incorrect watering, not enough lighting, and pest infestations are just a few of the problems you might encounter.

Of the three common problems I mentioned, incorrect watering should be the number one concern; it is the fastest way to kill these plants. Unfortunately, succulents placed indoors are more susceptible to overwatering.

Outside, the abundance of sunlight and adequate air circulation help prevent the plants from absorbing excess water.

Outdoors, most of the water evaporates, so even though the soil is soaked, it will dry out fast. By the time the plant has enough water, the soil will also be dry.

Indoors, the air circulation is very poor, and water from the soil does not evaporate quickly. With inadequate air circulation indoors, only a small amount of water evaporates from the soil. This is a challenge in addition to keeping succulents compact with limited indoor light.

When watering indoor succulent plants, you need to pay attention to every possible factor that can affect the amount of water the plant can access, including the length of time the roots are exposed to it. Your soil mixture, the size of the plant in relation to the container, and the amount of water you give can contribute to your success or failure.

Soil Mixture

Use a fast-draining soil mixture. The mixture can greatly affect the amount of absorbed water. In this case, you need a mixture that will allow water to drain through and not hold too much moisture. Soaking the soil well is not a good idea if you are using a soil mixture that is good at holding water. Create a mix that won't hold too much moisture by using the same materials you use outdoors, but with a more inorganic mix.

For example, if you use a 50 percent organic mix (two parts potting soil) and 50 percent inorganic mix (one part perlite and one part coarse sand) for outdoor succulents, change the proportion to one part organic mix and three parts inorganic mix. When you water, most of the water will drain through the pot, and whatever is absorbed won't be too much for the plants.

If you soak the soil well, and if most of the water is absorbed by the soil, the plant will obviously receive more than what it needs. That can happen especially in situations where the plant is small and the container is big.

Soil may remain wet for days if you use a lot of water, which is detrimental to the health of your succulents. Allowing them to sit in wet soil longer can cause root rot and cause them to absorb too much water.

The Challenge Of Growing Succulents Indoors

There are two major challenges that you will encounter when growing these plants indoors. The first challenge is giving them the right amount of water, and second, providing them adequate lighting.

1. Right Amount Of Water

The first challenge is watering indoor succulents without giving them too much. One wrong watering can destroy a plant, no matter how stable it is. As I mentioned earlier, the main factor that affects watering indoors is the lack of air circulation. The soil may remain wet longer. Therefore, giving your plants just enough water to satisfy their needs is important, as is providing an amount that will dry out fast.

You can water indoor succulents every two to three weeks or when the plants show signs of need. Ensure that the soil dries out in a day or two, and never let the plant sit in water. During winter, cut the watering down to once per month. Make sure the soil is completely dry in between watering. With the mixture mentioned earlier, you can water the pot well and allow the excess water to drain through.

2. Adequate Lighting

Not all succulents appreciate being indoors. Choosing succulents that will be happy inside your home or office will help. Colorful varieties are the fastest to elongate, turn pale, and grow smaller leaves when they do not receive enough light. This is called etiolation.

Most colorful succulents require full sun all day and are the quickest to elongate when placed indoors, so they may not be the best varieties to grow inside. This doesn't mean that you can't grow them at all. If you can find a location in your home with adequate lighting, like a window with bright light, some of them will do well. Otherwise, use grow lights. Closely observe how the plants behave. If they stretch out, then they are telling you that they are not receiving enough light.

There are some varieties that thrive better in low light. They will do well on windowsills with bright light. Examples of these succulent plants are *Haworthias, Gasterias, Sansevierias*.

What Your Plant Is Trying To Tell You

What Your Plant Is Trying To Tell You

Congratulations!
You've found the perfect spot that brings the best in your plants. They are healthy and happy.
Enjoy their beauty.

Make sure the soil is completely dry at this time. Otherwise, take the plant out from the pot and remove as much soil as possible. Do not expose to full sun.

The vibrant color of the plant will fade and will turn pale. This is a signal that they are not happy where they are. Provide light, but in a gradual manner. Start with morning sun.

The plant will benefit from a good soak. Water the soil thoroughly, and repeat several times. When the soil dries-out, and the plant is still wrinkly, water again until it plumps up. No need to change location.

What Your Plant Is Trying To Tell You

It's too hot for me. I'm protecting my young leaves. Oh, I also need water.

Wrinkly leaves with leather-like texture signify a lack of water. When it is too hot, the plant closes up its leaves to protect its delicate young ones. It will become dormant to survive.

I am searching for more light.

When the light is not enough, some plants will stretch out to look for more. The leaves spread out, resulting in a bigger space in between. The plant loses its compactness and may look unsightly.

Ouch! The bugs are feasting on me

You'll notice the new leaves in the middle will start curling up. Other areas will have uneven red bite marks. You might also see some white cotton-like patches on the leaves and stems. Mealybugs can damage your plant. Spray with 70 percent isopropyl alcohol and rinse with water.

The light is too strong for me. Can you please move me somewhere cool?

Not all plants are happy in full sun. Some thrive better in low-light locations. Transfer to a spot with bright light but still protected from harsh sunlight. You can also use shade cloth for protection.

What Your Plant Is Trying To Tell You

When some plant is severely dehydrated, it does not have enough cushion to protect it from completely drying up or turning crisp from prolonged exposure to the intense heat of the sun. In this case, the plant is less likely to survive.

As more water gets absorbed, their translucent window gets more swollen and their outer leaf cover becomes thinner. This one looks like a blister that is about to pop. Remove from the soil, and keep it dry.

Remove the plant right away from its sunny location. Remove the rotten leaves. If the soil is still wet, remove them too. Some parts of the plant can still be saved by removing it from the source of water.

The fine whitish-gray powdery film on the leaves of some succulents is their protective coating. It acts as a sunscreen protecting them from the heat of the sun. Avoid touching it.

What Your Plant Is Trying To Tell You
And What You Should Do

I'm okay.
These dry leaves are normal

As new leaves grow, old leaves die, and it's normal. You can remove the dry leaves by hand or using long tweezers. When left unattended, they can become breeding grounds for insects.

I don't get enough water through my roots, so I'm getting it from the air.

Roots above the soil are called aerial roots. They can receive moisture from the humid air. Sometimes, they use it for support by clinging to a surface to prevent them from falling over.

My leaves are so delicate.
Please handle me with care.

Plants like Aeonium have delicate leaves that can easily get bruised when handled. It may not disappear and may look unpleasant, but it won't kill the plant. Over time, they will grow healthy, unblemished leaves.

Someone bit me.
Look for the culprit!

The succulent leaves of these plants are very tempting to snails and slugs as well as other pests present in the garden. Controlling these pests, removing weeds, and adding rocks and pebbles around your plant can help.

Don't give me water during midday and try to avoid my leaves when you water.

When the temperature is mild, or, if it is windy, water beads that settles on the leaves will not cause a problem. But, when it is too hot, it can magnify the heat of the sun and can cause sunburn.

I had too much water and I need more light.

To check if the plant had too much water, look at the direction where the tip of the leaves are pointing. Instead of upwards, like the compact rosette, they point downwards as they expand to hold more.

I had too much water. My leaves are getting heavy and they are falling-off.

There's a way to tell if the plant had too much water. Their leaves can tell. They would look so bloated. Over time, they will become heavy and will fall off. Rescue the plant ASAP. Propagate intact leaves.

I survived fluid overload and sunburn. Can you see my new leaves?

Plants can be saved from severe damages from absorbing too much water and severe sun damage when the problem is detected early. Ugly marks will soon be replaced with beautiful new growths.

Frost tender succulents can get damaged when exposed to temperatiures below freezing (32 °F) cover plants with frost cloth when decline of temp is anticipated

The stored moisture inside their leaves can freeze and destroy their storage cells. Identify which plants are frost hardy and which ones are frost tender. The longer the exposure, the more damage occurs.

Despite being overwatered, You can still save some of the non-affected parts. Remove the damaged leaves and plant green parts as cuttings.Over-watered, undamaged leaves can be propagated.

When the plants are not fully rooted, they are very delicate. Even the light coming through a glass window or reflective surfaces can burn them. Move the plant few inches away from the source of heat.

My Gift For You

Thank you for reading my first book. It is my utmost desire to help you gain enough knowledge and understanding of these unique plants. I wish nothing more for you than to have confidence in growing these plants and to truly enjoy this amazing hobby.

I assure you, as you take care of these plants, they will take care of you. They will help you keep your sanity and make you happy. They can be your companion and help you temporarily forget your worries. The best stress reliever, I must say.

Planting succulents is cheaper than therapy. Take your time when you are with your plants, and enjoy the peace and comfort they bring.

Know, also, the great impact you can contribute to our Mother Nature. By growing succulents, you can help turn this planet a bit greener every day, if not colorful.

Now that you know what makes these plants unique, I hope you will use their strengths to your advantage. Try preventing failure by avoiding their weaknesses. I encourage you to try practicing what you've learned.

Look at your plants with a different set of eyes.

Feel them; understand what they are trying to convey.

Lastly, don't forget to enjoy this amazing hobby.

Happy succulent planting!

Theresa

Acknowledgments

I am truly grateful to a lot of people who either inspired me, motivated me through their kind and encouraging words, or just simply listened to my unending chatter about succulents.

To Enrico Esteban, who gifted me my first succulent arrangement and played a major role in my successful journey with succulents. Who's a cactus-collector for more than 30 years, and an Agri-Bus graduate of UP Diliman. He saw my great interest in these drought-smart plants and guided me. He later became my personal consultant, nurtured my creative brain, and believed in what I can do. Most of all, he built me ledges to organize our garden.

To my Dolidnon Sa America family, especially to Mela Palacios, who inspired me through her succulent garden, Dr. Wilgie Mae Tabligan Serna for helping me with my website, Zenny Palacios Gepilano who helped design our facade, and to Caroline Palacios and Liezl Barroca Tiu for celebrating the milestones with me.

Special thanks to Benjamin Ramos, for taking the beautiful photographs of my arrangements.

To my colleagues at Anaheim Regional Medical Center, Med-Surg Telemetry Unit, especially to Rick Domingo, for installing my wall frames, and to Leilanie Baker for introducing me to the shipping business.

Thanks to my dear friends Melanie Gimay and Dinah Castro who stood by me from the very beginning and helped out in any way they could, making every experience a memorable one. Either from setting up my first fair to packing my shipments until the wee hours of the morning.

To all the subscribers of my YouTube channel, followers of my Facebook Page, Instagram, and members of the Facebook group, Chopstick and Succulents Global, especially Brenda Sendin, for bringing me to her best-kept-secret nurseries and sharing her expertise in succulent plants identification.

To Hazelyn Guerrero of Guerrero Farms, Philippines, George Nursery in Compton and Oscar Vargas and Myra Jimenez of GreenTouch Nursery in Bellflower ; thank you for your beautiful and very colorful succulents.

Website: https://chopstickandsucculents.com/
Facebook Page:https://www.facebook.com/chopstickandsucculents.org/
Instagram: https://www.instagram.com/chopstick_and_succulents/

RESOURCES

https://en.wikipedia.org/wiki/Succulent_plant
https://en.wikipedia.org/wiki/Aeonium
http://www.crassulaceae.ch/de/artikel?akID=63
https://www.livescience.com/5793-plants-recognize-rivals-fight-play-nice-siblings.html
https://worldofsucculents.com/?genera=echeveria
https://wimastergardener.org/article/whats-in-a-name-understanding-botanical-or-latin-names/
https://www.ncbi.nlm.nih.gov/pmc/articles/PMC2712704/
http://www.bellaonline.com/articles/art69526.asp
https://worldofsucculents.com/understanding-succulent-plant-names/
https://serc.carleton.edu/integrate/teaching_materials/food_supply/student_materials/805
https://fyi.extension.wisc.edu/sewmg/files/2018/03/MAJOR-FAMILIES-AND-GENERA-OF-SUCCU-
LENT-PLANTS-3-5
-18-handout.pdf
https://worldofsucculents.com/browse-succulents-genus/
https://en.wikipedia.org/wiki/Aeonium
https://kids.frontiersin.org/article/10.3389/frym.2017.00058
https://en.wikipedia.org/wiki/Portulacaria_afra
https://en.wikipedia.org/wiki/Aloe
https://en.wikipedia.org/wiki/Aloe
https://www.haworthia.com/
https://en.wikipedia.org/wiki/Haworthia
https://en.wikipedia.org/wiki/Euphorbia
https://en.wikipedia.org/wiki/Kalanchoe
https://en.wikipedia.org/wiki/Sedum
https://en.wikipedia.org/wiki/Senecio
https://en.wikipedia.org/wiki/Sempervivum
https://en.wikipedia.org/wiki/Sansevieria
https://en.wikipedia.org/wiki/Graptopetalum
https://en.wikipedia.org/wiki/Succulent_plant
https://ohioline.osu.edu/factsheet/anr-36
https://en.wikipedia.org/wiki/Soil_microbiology
https://en.wikipedia.org/wiki/Xerophyte
https://www.saps.org.uk/saps-associates/browse-q-and-a/164-can-you-give-me-some-information-on-xe-
rophytes
https://en.wikipedia.org/wiki/Xerophyte
https://www.usgs.gov/special-topic/water-science-school/science/evapotranspiration-and-water-cycle?qt-sci-
ence_cen
ter_objects=0#qt-science_center_objects
http://southernlivingplants.com/plant-care/article/understanding-sun-exposur
https://en.m.wikipedia.org/wiki/Euphorbiaceae
https://www.google.com/amp/s/www.zmescience.com/other/feature-post/beginners-guide-naming-spe-
cies-latin/amp/
https://worldofsucculents.com/?genera=kalanchoe
https://www.sciencedirect.com/science/article/pii/S2405844017301007
https://hortnews.extension.iastate.edu/2008/2-6/CultivarOrVariety.html

CPSIA information can be obtained
at www.ICGtesting.com
Printed in the USA
LVHW071046250621
691133LV00006B/302